1995

Women
& Social
Change

Women
& Social
Change

NONPROFITS
AND SOCIAL POLICY

EDITED BY
FELICE DAVIDSON
PERLMUTTER

National Association of Social Workers
Washington, DC

Linda Beebe, *Executive Editor*
Nancy Winchester, *Editorial Services Director*
Wolf Publications, Inc., *Project Manager*
Patricia Lipscomb, *Copy Editor*
Susan Harris, *Proofreader*
Marina Rota, *Proofreader*
Schroeder Indexing Service, *Indexer*

Library of Congress Cataloging-in-Publication Data
Women & social change : nonprofits and social policy / edited by Felice
Davidson Perlmutter.
    p. cm.
    Includes bibliographical references (p.) and index.
    ISBN 0-87101-239-1
    1. Women--Services for--Cross-cultural studies. 2. Social work
with women--Cross-cultural studies. 3. Nonprofit organizations-
-Cross-cultural studies. 4. Women social reformers--Cross-cultural
studies. 5. Women--Societies and clubs--Cross-cultural studies.
I. Perlmutter, Felice Davidson. II. Title: Women and social change.
HV1444.W65 1994
362.83—dc20   94-23149
                                                     CIP

Printed in the United States of America

To my daughters who face new challenges—
To my husband and son who face new challenges—
as we all grow and learn.

Contents

Preface

Women's interests and concerns have elicited attention in various nations, primarily as a result of the increased activity on the part of women themselves. Not only have women sought to improve their immediate situation through the provision of an array of services, but they have also coupled this concern with a clear agenda for broader social and political change.

At the same time, given the dramatic changes in social, political, and economic systems of many countries in Europe, there is increasing interest in nonprofit social services organizations. Eastern European nations are struggling to develop a nonprofit social services sector, and many welfare states are examining the unique role of nonprofit organizations within the shadow of the welfare state.

This book, composed of invitational chapters written by experts in nonprofits and women's services in seven countries, examines the formation of nonprofit alternative social services organizations that developed to meet the needs of women in societies with different social–political contexts. The formation of these organizations was caused by the failure of broader society to address these needs. A particular focus of this book is to help the reader understand the role of these nonprofit organizations in relation to meeting special human needs, developing social policy, and defining the relationship between nonprofits and the public sector.

This book should meet the interests of several diverse groups. First, women's studies programs are expanding their interests as they examine social policies and social programs both in the United States and abroad. The various chapters call attention to the similarities of issues faced by women in different societal contexts. Although the case study of a particular organization is the focus of each chapter, all the discussions are placed in a social policy context; a central criterion for inclusion in this book was the involvement of the selected women's group in system change.

Second, scholars of nonprofit organizations are concerned with the diverse activity in this arena. Their number is dramatically increasing as evidenced by the following developments: Important national and international associations that attract scholars from various disciplines have emerged; several academic programs that focus on the nonprofit sector have become important centers of excellence; and, finally, several scholarly journals are being published in this field. All these developments have played a central role in the growth of nonprofit scholarship, and a serious body of research has emerged.

Third, alternative social services are of special interest to the profession of social work because these organizations focus on empowerment, ideology, and social change. Schools of social work are becoming more interested in gender issues, and more attention is being paid to women's concerns not only in the social policy and practice sequences, but also as a specialization. Furthermore, administration, policy, and planning sequences are particularly interested in the design of alternative service systems and their relation to social policy, advocacy, and change.

Part I of this volume provides a conceptual overview of issues and developments in relation to the nonprofit sector and to the structure and function of alternative organizations. Part II presents the case studies of women's organizations in seven countries with a focus on issues related to mission, governance, leadership, advocacy, services, and inter-organizational relations.

The important roles played by the numerous actors in these nonprofit alternative organizations that serve women's interests merit special acknowledgment.

—Felice Davidson Perlmutter

PART I
Conceptual Underpinnings

CHAPTER ONE

Women's Alternative Organizations

Felice Davidson Perlmutter

All societies have social problems and emerging social needs that have not been addressed; our focus here is on social change undertaken by groups of women. Since the 1960s, across the world, there has been an increase in social activism initiated by women. This is not a chance phenomenon, nor did it occur as a result of broad societal interest. Rather, it is the direct result of women seeking empowerment and organizing themselves, as highlighted in "alternative organizations (AOs)," the emergence of women's movements. The form through which this activity often takes place, within the context of the nonprofit sector, is a structural arrangement most compatible with the values and missions of the women's groups (Perlmutter, 1988). These organizations have been created to meet needs that society as a whole has not yet acknowledged. They are risk-taking groups that deal with social problems not yet recognized or accepted by the larger society, and they are based on "precarious values," in contrast to the "secure values" that underpin traditional organizations (Clark, 1956). Secure and precarious values will vary in different societies. In the United States a secure value is the assumption that all citizens will work; a precarious value is illustrated by the belief that women have a right to choice.

AOs view themselves as departing significantly from the broader society not only in their values but also in their mission, governance, and method of operation. A high premium is placed on participatory, egalitarian governance (Grossman & Morgenbesser, 1980). Limiting the size of the organization is considered essential to provide personalized service and to prevent bureaucratization (Kanter & Zurcher, 1973; Rothschild-Whitt, 1979). In addition, a unique relationship exists among the personnel involved in the service. Not only does the professional work side by side with the volunteer to provide service in an egalitarian setting, but often the volunteer has been a former recipient of that service.

Clarifying organizational mission and retaining control of development are critical issues for alternative organizations in the nonprofit sector, because the organizations depend on external sources for funding. Maintaining autonomy can be especially difficult when government is a major supplier of resources and when the organization is involved in meeting broad social policy objectives. The danger of goal displacement is always great because the alternative organization is often at risk of compromising its mission, its values, its structure, and its program to survive.

This book examines alternative women's organizations in seven countries and explores similarities and differences. It is of interest to examine these developments on a cross-cultural basis, because they have evolved in different economic and political systems. The central criterion for inclusion in this volume was that the organization have a dual mission: to promote social change and to provide related social services. The case study was used for analysis because it provides an opportunity to examine the condition of women from the perspective of the broader societal context, as well as within the internal organizational environment.

Each of the national case studies in this book addresses issues shared by the women's groups. These issues, presented within varied societal contexts, include

- the social problem that stimulated the formation of the alternative social service organization

- a description of the organization, its mission, and underlying values

- the governance mechanism and the relationship of the staff and the consumer of the service to the policy-making process

- the social–economic–political environment

- how the organization obtains resources

- how the organization deals with controversy

- the intersystem relationships of this organization within the voluntary sector and with the public sector

- the organization's chances for survival.

The authors then provide their unique analyses, interpretations, and conclusions concerning a particular organization and its relationship to broader public policy issues.

It is important to highlight the fact that each society is based on a different set of political and economic realities, and accordingly, the women's movement and alternative organizations in each country reflect a different set of assumptions and a different policy frame. The unique language and constructs endemic to a country have been retained; however, the basic content of each case study is universal.

A broad range of social and political conditions frame these case studies. The United States, on the one hand, represents the most individualistic society, with few social supports available for nonprofit organizations in general and for AOs in particular. Similarly, but under a completely different set of circumstances, Croatia represents the reality of many nations in the former Socialist orbit, whose governments do not provide resources to sustain these organizations. And in Israel there is no public support for the alternative group. In contrast, the case studies from Australia, Denmark, New Zealand, and Sweden provide variations on the role of the state in supporting alternative programs, with differences in the ability of the alternative organization to retain its autonomy and integrity while utilizing public resources. The consequences of these differing realities are both interesting and important for professionals, policymakers, and researchers in the nonprofit sector.

As noted above, the case studies presented from Israel, Croatia, and the United States have a common thread in the lack of public funds to support them. The American group has been most effective in retaining its dual commitment to both social change and service provision, by developing new service strategies that support a social change function. In the face of complex external economic and political pressures, and overwhelmed by service demands, the Israeli organization has experienced serious erosion of its ability to focus on commitment to social change; however, such commitment remains part of the organization's agenda. And Croatia's situation is certainly unique because it is a nation at war. However, despite the Croatian organization being overwhelmed by the ongoing assault of emergencies, it has managed to articulate a long-range agenda that addresses broad social policy concerns regarding the status of women.

It should be noted that many of the AOs have managed to hold on to a unique set of values, commitment to the mission of the organization, absence of hierarchy, participatory management, and sense of collectivism. However, it also should be noted that these characteristics have not been sustained easily and that the organizations have a history of conflict and struggle to retain these unique qualities.

The commitment to social change, shared by all of these groups, presents a complex challenge. It appears that in societies with a welfare state orientation (such as Australia, Denmark, New Zealand, and Sweden), much of the original platform of AOs has become public policy, and these groups have moved in from the fringe and are less involved with social policy and social change. However, the problems faced by women in these nations are far from resolved, and a dilemma exists as to how to infuse or ignite a social activist position in a generally supportive policy environment. Another concern must be identified in the future stability of AOs in a welfare state environment. As welfare states experience various degrees of fiscal crisis, and as many of their governments explore privatization as a policy option, the question arises as to whether these women's groups will be more vulnerable than groups with a longer history of institutionalization and based on more broadly accepted social values such as family service agencies.

The women's agenda remains active throughout the world; unfortunately, the work is far from being completed. Many of the conditions that led to the emergence of women's movements and women's organizations still exist, and these organizations will continue to serve an important role in societal change.

Alternative women's organizations have a rich and diverse story to tell, dealing with issues of democratization, human need, and social change— concerns shared by all AOs (Wilkerson, 1988). The following chapters should provide useful material for students of social policy, administration, and management and for students of women's issues, as well as for scholars of AOs and nonprofit organizations.

References

Clark, B. R. (1956). Organizational adaptation and precarious values. *American Sociological Review, 21,* 327–336.

Grossman, B., & Morgenbesser, M. (1980). Alternative social service settings: Opportunities for social work education. *Journal of Humanics, 8,* 59–76.

Kanter, R. M., & Zurcher, L. A. (1973). Evaluating alternatives and alternative valuing. *Journal of Applied Behavioral Science, 9*(2/3), 381–397.

Perlmutter, F. D. (1988). *Alternative social agencies: Administrative strategies.* New York: Haworth Press.

Rothschild-Whitt, J. (1979). Conditions for democracy: Making participatory organizations work. In J. Case & R. Taylor (Eds.), *Co-ops, communes and collectives.* New York: Pantheon Books.

Wilkerson, A. E. (1988). Epilogue. In *Alternative social agencies: Administrative strategies* (pp. 119–128). New York: Haworth Press.

CHAPTER TWO

The Nonprofit Sector

Felice Davidson Perlmutter

This chapter is intended for readers who are not familiar with nonprofits. It is included in this book because alternative organizations in general, and women's agencies in particular, are a part of the nonprofit world. Many of the issues concerning nonprofits are of importance to both women's groups and alternative organizations. This discussion is presented in the context of the profession of social work (Macarov, 1991). Readers familiar with the literature on nonprofits can proceed to Part II: Cross-National Case Studies.

This chapter discusses the nonprofit sector from a management perspective. First, it describes the emergence of the entity identified as the nonprofit sector, with a focus on its unique characteristics. Second, it identifies selected issues that are critical to the management of this sector. Third, it highlights some critical policy issues that concern nonprofits in the United States.

What Is the Nonprofit Sector?

Historical Background

It is fitting to include a discussion of the nonprofit sector in this volume because the origins of this sector can be traced to the founding of the United States, when voluntary social service organizations were established to meet human needs. This arrangement supported a fundamental tenet of our society: the belief in a laissez-faire form of government (Wilensky & Lebeaux, 1958). This political philosophy, based on the assumption "that government that governs best governs least" served to encourage the dichotomy between the public and voluntary sectors.

An extensive system of social services agencies was developed in the form of voluntary associations, governed by volunteer boards of directors (deGrazia, 1957). Historically, these charitable organizations were organized primarily under sectarian auspices, because religious groups traditionally have been responsible for meeting the needs of their members (Leiby, 1987). It should be noted that many of these early social services organizations shared an important dimension with alternative agencies in that the needs they sought to serve were not accepted by the broader society through public programs. For example, services for children and their families were provided by social services agencies that were nonprofits.

The social services groups developed a unique profile: (1) They had a central purpose or mission that was related to a social need or problem; (2) profit from the activity was not a consideration; (3) the agencies depended on voluntary labor both for policy development and for program administration; and (4) the financial base was based on "voluntary contributions."

Definitions/Descriptors

The social services were the earliest form of nonprofits in the United States, but they did not remain unique in their organizational arrangements. In 1835 Alexis de Tocqueville was struck by the pervasive pattern of voluntary association and volunteer activity in general in the United States: "Americans of all ages, all conditions, and all dispositions constantly form associations.... Wherever at the head of some new undertaking you see the government in France, or a man of rank in England, in the United States you will be sure to find an association" (de Tocqueville, 1961, pp. 128–129).

Indeed in 1984, 821,000 nonprofits were in existence in the United States (Hodgkinson & Weitzman, 1990), representing a wide array of interests and functions. These features have led to the creation of the concept of "the nonprofit sector."

Filer (1990) identified a broad spectrum of groups that are included in the framework of the nonprofit sector:

The practice of attending to community needs outside of government has profoundly shaped American society and its institutional framework. While in most other countries, major social institutions, such as universities, hospitals, schools, libraries, museums and social welfare agencies are state-run and state-funded, in the United States many of the same organizations are privately controlled and voluntarily supported. The institutional landscape of America is, in fact, teeming with nongovernmental, noncommercial organizations, all the way from some of the world's leading educational and cultural institutions to local garden clubs, from politically powerful national associations to block associations—literally millions of groups in all. This vast and varied array is...part of the very fabric of American life. It reflects a national belief in the philosophy of pluralism and in the profound importance to society of individual initiative. (p. 70)

The nonprofit sector consists of a conglomerate of organizations with diverse purposes and social functions, ranging from libraries to art museums, from nationally based organizations to community-based groups. They share the critical characteristics of social services. First, all nonprofit organizations have a central purpose or mission as they seek to serve society. Second, service—not economic gain—is an expectation. Third, nonprofits depend on voluntary labor for developing organizational policy and implementing their programs. And last, nonprofits depend on voluntary donations.

Tax Exemptions and Tax Benefits as Social Policy

One final, but critical, aspect of nonprofits requires special emphasis: the issue of tax policy (Scrivner, 1990). The importance of tax policy is illustrated by the definition of a new type of nonprofit organization developed in the early 1980s called "independent sector." This organizational category serves the critical function of including as an entity all the diverse groups and organizations that have a special tax status: "The independent sector consists of those nonprofit organizations that are defined as 501(c)(3) and 501(c)(4) organizations under the federal tax code for tax-exempt organizations" (Hodgkinson & Weitzman, 1990, p. 41).

This brief discussion of tax policy and its rationale from a historical perspective covers both the tax exemption status of organizations and tax benefits for individual taxpayers. In regard to tax exemption, the development of the early social services under religious auspices is most relevant. With the separation of church and state ensured by the First Amendment of the Constitution, the sponsoring bodies of social services agencies, through their boards of directors, had total authority to determine the nature and framework of an organization's constitution, bylaws, and services. To facilitate the development of this voluntary system, and based on the rationale that if the voluntary agencies did not provide these services the public sector would have to do so (Scrivner, 1990), these social services agencies and their property were declared tax exempt. Over time, these agencies became very dependent on these tax benefits to maintain their financial solvency.

In the development of the second major tax strategy—tax benefits for individuals—the United States looked to England for its social policy approach:

> In 1601 the king and Parliament enacted the Statute of Charitable Trusts and Uses which clarified and strengthened the power of citizens and associations to endow or support helping agencies without going through the machinery of government. They conceived the law to help rich people make large benefactions, usually in the form of land, to establish an almshouse, hospital or school. Previously, the wealthy could have given the money to the church, which presumably would follow their wishes and administer the agency in perpetuity. The new statute made it possible for them to enter into a legal contract with a specific group of trustees and its successors. It stimulated voluntary philanthropy. (Leiby, 1987, p. 759)

Thus, in addition to the tax exemptions granted to social agencies, tax benefits for the wealthy who contributed to these agencies were also instituted.

Since the 1980s, with the Reagan and Bush administrations, the fiscal environment has radically changed, greatly diminishing the historical practice of tax supports as social policy. This change was precipitated by the federal government's withdrawal from contracting for social services, which forced many nonprofits to seek new sources of income. Thus, profit-making ventures were increasingly attempted to compensate for the loss of public money (Adams & Perlmutter, 1991; Perlmutter & Adams, 1990).

Special attention has been paid to the concept of the unrelated business income tax (UBIT), a policy Congress put forth in 1950 in the Internal Revenue Code, seeking to narrow the range of tax exemptions for nonprofits (Rose-Ackerman, 1990). To be considered tax exempt, income produced by a charity has to be directly related to its mission or purpose. As private enterprises increasingly enter the social services arena, the small business lobby has become more vigilant in regard to UBITs. In 1984, the Small Business Administration published a report entitled "Unfair Competition by Nonprofit Corporations with Small Business: An Issue for the 1980s." And at a White House Conference for Small Business in 1986, more than 20,000 small business representatives ranked competition with nonprofits as one of the most significant issues they faced at the time. This issue is far from resolved (Perlmutter, Adams, & Kramer, 1990).

In regard to individual charitable contributions, all nonprofits have also been affected by the change in the Tax Reform Act of 1986. Charitable contributions sharply dropped as the tax rate for individuals with high incomes was dramatically reduced; apparently the loss of tax deductions reduced the incentives for charitable contributions.

Management Roles of Nonprofit Executives

Although they differ in their purposes, functions, and target populations, the nonprofits share commonalities within the management arena. For the purposes of this discussion, I have selected issues of general concern that also are discussed in the case studies in this book: executive leadership, policy and planning, boards of directors, human resources, and financial management.

Executive Leadership

Executive leadership is a complex topic that has been discussed from many perspectives. This discussion of leadership in nonprofits focuses on the ethical dimensions of—an area that has received relatively little attention, yet is of critical importance. In fact, O'Neill (1992) argued cogently that this may be the most important element in nonprofit administration because managers have

unique responsibilities as outlined below:

Developing, shaping and articulating values—values not only of the members of the organization but also of the larger society...

Motivating and managing workers without using economic incentives ([for example,] nonprofits that rely heavily or exclusively on volunteer labor, advocacy organizations that pay extremely low wages)...

Managing organizations that provide services that clients cannot effectively test or monitor ([for example,] day care centers, nursing homes, hospitals, mental health clinics)...

Managing organizations in which there is no clear financial or political bottom line...

Interacting extensively with a board. (pp. 203–204)

O'Neill thus called attention to those aspects of the nonprofit organization that make it unique. He highlighted the increased commitment of both the clients served and the volunteers and professionals who work in these systems for little or no pay because of their belief in the organization's values and objectives.

Organizations in the nonprofit sector are responsive to conditions in society that are not being addressed (Perlmutter, 1988b). Quite often they represent minority positions and unpopular causes; in these cases, the issue of values and ideology is central, and it is all the more urgent that the leadership focus on ethical issues and responsibilities. Whereas in traditional organizations, professional, organizational, and personal or ideological competencies are valued in that order, in alternative organizations the situation is reversed and the ideological commitments take precedence (Perlmutter, 1988a).

The ethical behavior of executives has been questioned in the past few years (Gaul & Borowski, 1993); unfortunately, there has been an abuse of public trust in major nonprofit organizations. This is particularly troublesome in a sector where, in O'Neill's words, "the possible feeling that the sector that does good needn't worry about being good.... The organizational complexity of the American nonprofit sector, and the importance of all ethical considerations in an increasingly amoral society, are grounds for giving more attention to this topic" (pp. 211–212). It should be noted that attention has been given to administrative and professional ethics in the social work literature (Levy, 1979).

Policy and Planning

The second important management role of nonprofit executives concerns policy and planning. Both policy formulation and planning have commanded increasing attention since the 1960s, when social planning became a distinct profession. The importance of policy and planning has increased in the past decade, as resources have become limited while problems to be addressed have multiplied. Although in women's organizations the planning process is inextricably linked to the commitment to participatory democracy and self-management, the expertise needed to conduct policy and planning is emphasized here:

> Strategic planning and policy formulation are the methods... people use to decide and then to act upon such fundamental identity issues as: who and what our organization is and is not; how our organization fits into and attempts to shape its particular environment; how we cope with changes in environmental influences (and in turn how we influence our environment); what we value, and what ... line of endeavor we are in. Strategic planning and policy formulation set parameters or limits, within which day-to-day decisions will be made. They help the board of directors and the staff bring order out of confusion. (Gies, Ott, & Shafritz, 1990, p. 138)

Traditionally, the policy and planning process is viewed as the place for rational behavior within organizations. Policy has been defined as "program intent which reflects decisions made on the basis of principle with a supporting rationale," in contrast to politics, which is viewed as "the action of interest groups affecting and affected by the policy" (Perlmutter, 1980, p. 58). Gummer (1990) linked the two together, arguing that the planning process represents the allocation of values and hence is a political process. In his discussion of planning as a strategy in nonprofit organizations, Stone (1989) linked the planning process to the nature of the funding environment, lending support to Gummer's view.

It is essential that organizational leaders become schooled in the technical processes necessary for formulating broad policy directions and implementing a strategic planning process. These processes are especially important in small organizations where the executive and board are both involved. Bryson (1988) viewed strategic planning as the link between the mission of the organization and its environment, which helps move the organization from broad policy choices to implementation.

Boards of Directors

The role and function of the board of directors is directly related to the policy and planning process and is a major aspect of the executive's job in nonprofit organizations, for traditional and alternative systems alike. However, in traditional nonprofit organizations, this relationship is especially complex for several reasons: First, the administrators of policy and planning are hired by the organization's board of directors; second, the board has the power to fire them; and third, the administrative professional is broadly focused on delivering the service that implements the agency's mission, whereas the board members' expertise is usually in specific legal or fiscal matters.

Although the conventional understanding is that the board is responsible for determining policies and the administrator is responsible for implementing these policies, in reality the process is far from cut-and-dried. Most often, the administrator is critical in determining the nature and extent of the relationship with the board.

In contrast to the administrator, who is involved with the agency on a full-time basis, the board members are volunteers who have primary responsibilities elsewhere. The administrator provides agency statistics, interprets client–consumer–patient needs, discusses program options, and provides information on funding possibilities. Thus, board members are dependent in their decision making on the material supplied by the administrator, and consequently the administrator is very much a part of the policy-making process. Although the relationship works because a balance is maintained (Kramer, 1969), Gurin (1978) suggested that the relationship between policy analysis and management "is never settled for all time but involves a continuous process of negotiation" (p. 296).

An effective administrator will be proactive and innovative, responding to the changing needs and conditions in the environment. An effective administrator will not only serve as an advocate with the board, but will stimulate the board to advocate for the organization in the broader political arena.

A study of boards of nonprofit agencies found that although "being deeply involved in strategic planning, developing a common vision of the organization's activities, and operating according to the guidelines for good meeting management" created positive perceptions with top management, the board's involvement with, and responsibility for, fiscal management and solvency is minimal (Bradshaw, Murray, & Wolpin, 1992, p. 247). Thus, it appears that even in the areas of policy and planning that are most closely related to board responsibilities, the administrative or executive leadership remains central in traditional nonprofits and is so perceived by both board presidents and administrators or executives themselves (Heimovics & Herman, 1990).

Human Resources

Organizational policies are implemented by the people who work in the organization at all levels and in all capacities. The levels range from upper-level administrators, to middle managers and supervisors, to frontline staff. The diverse roles can be professional, volunteer, paraprofessional, clerical, food service, and maintenance. In traditional nonprofits, the executive director is responsible for the quality of the agency's performance; hence, the performance of the people in the system is an executive responsibility, albeit delegated.

An effective staff is one that understands and is committed to the mission of the organization, and it is the executive who creates the climate and makes this commitment possible. Peters and Waterman (1983) highlighted the importance of each individual in the organization being seen as a source of ideas and the root source of quality and productivity. Equal attention must be given to all levels in the organization, from the middle managers (Perlmutter, 1983) to volunteers (Perlmutter, 1984).

Human resources management is becoming increasingly complex. There is increasing competition for trained professionals because nonprofits are competing with profit-making organizations that have entered the human services arena. Also, salaries in nonprofits are lower than in the public or for-profit sectors, exacerbating the problem of not only attracting but retaining competent staff. Furthermore, the unionization of nonprofit organizations requires special administrative expertise (Alexander, 1987). And finally, burnout is a phenomenon that is increasing in nonprofits that address complex social problems or operate within an environment of severe fiscal constraints (Harvey & Raider, 1984). There is no question that the management of human resources is a critical executive function, whether it is assumed by a designated leader or by a management committee.

Financial Management

Obtaining financial resources has always been an important activity in the nonprofit sector. In the early years of social services organizations, boards of directors assumed this responsibility, and fundraising among wealthy board members and their contacts was the primary source of funds (Perlmutter, 1990). As funding streams became more complex—first with the emergence of United Way and other foundations and then with the advent of government grants and contracts—financial management became a critical executive function in all nonprofit organizations. It is only in recent times, a period characterized as one of "tight money," that this function has come under close scrutiny (Gummer, 1990):

> The roughly 30-year period from the New Deal through the Great Society was clearly one in which the governmental culture was in the ascendancy. This period represented the greatest expansion in social spending in the country's history and witnessed a dramatic increase in the overall scope and importance of government.... By contrast, the period from the early 1970s to the present has been one in which the influence of the business community has achieved its highest level in this century.
>
> During the ascendancy of the governmental culture, social policy was viewed as a positive device for promoting the well-being of all citizens. The emphasis was on innovative programs and the use of government funds to uncover and remediate previously neglected areas of social and economic malfunctioning. By contrast, the growing importance of the business culture has shifted the emphasis to businesslike management practices and fiscal probity. (p. 33)

Not only has the availability of money decreased in recent times, but various needs have increased, and the pressures on executives in the financial arena are overwhelming (Perlmutter & Adams, 1994). These financial pressures can be linked to tax policy because, as noted earlier, the tax benefits that were of great importance to nonprofits are being continuously challenged and eroded.

Critical Policy Issues

A discussion of the nonprofit sector in the United States must address two critical issues. The first concerns the assignment of responsibility for provision of services; the second concerns the function of nonprofits and voluntarism in a democratic society.

The United States is unique in its view that government should not bear responsibility for the provision of social and cultural services. In all other industrialized nations, governments have assumed responsibility for a broad array of services—for example, in the arts, education, and the social services. In the United States, the nonprofit sector was established to provide services that the government did not consider its responsibility; this situation has led to the most extensive and sophisticated nonprofit sector in the world. As a result, the nonprofit sector in the United States is often looked to as a model, especially among developing nations and nations in Eastern Europe that are seeking alternatives to the inadequate services provided by their unstable governments.

But it is precisely this rationale for the existence of the U.S. nonprofit sector that creates dilemmas for our society. Under the Reagan and Bush administrations, the philosophy of privatization and voluntarism reified the nonprofit sector, as was symbolically demonstrated by President Bush's symbol, "a thousand points of light." This total and excessive reliance on the nonprofit sector has in fact led to the diminution of the service sector, and inadequacies are now faced both in the public and the nonprofit spheres.

Denmark provides an excellent contrast to the United States, because the Danish nonprofit sector is viewed as an extension of government, serving a public policy function and receiving public funding. Thus, opportunity is available for innovative programs that meet the special needs of society. In his chapter in this book, K. K. Klausen suggests that the recent introduction of private, voluntary and nonprofit organizations in the social welfare services in Denmark, which at first sight may seem to challenge the welfare state, is in fact no new phenomenon; that the organizations starting up at the fringe of society quickly become a part of the modern negotiated economy; that their services constitute an integrated part of the public system as an institutionalized paragovernmental provision of specific welfare services; and that this is rooted in tradition and in a practice of mutual recognition and dependency. Being nongovernmental, voluntary based and nonprofit oriented, their organization and specific assets, however, allow nonprofit organizations to play an important and distinct role in the distribution of the welfare mix, in the sense that they function both as alternatives and as supplementary to the pure public welfare provision regarding specific social problems. According to Perlmutter (1971), in Denmark nonprofits are assured of government money, and they retain the right to self-determination. It is interesting to note that the issue of public funding of nonprofits has created major policy debates in the United States, with a focus on the ability of the nonprofit to retain autonomy.

The second critical issue concerning nonprofits relates to the important function they serve in a democratic society. Nonprofits and voluntarism offer citizens the opportunity to express their needs and interests, apart from those of government. In fact, Berger and Neuhaus

(1990) argued that nonprofits play a mediating function that is critical in a democratic society. Accordingly, "public policy should protect and foster mediating structures, and wherever possible ... utilize mediating structures for the realization of social purposes" (pp. 15–16). This point is extremely important when one looks at nondemocratic societies that are struggling to develop mechanisms that will make them democratic.

It is clear that nonprofits play a unique and critical role in our society. However, it is important to recognize their strengths and limitations, both to develop social policy and to provide leadership that will maximize the nonprofit sector contribution to a civil society.

References

Adams, C. T., & Perlmutter, F. D. (1991). Commercial venturing and the transformation of America's social welfare agencies. *Nonprofit and Voluntary Sector Quarterly, 20*(1), 25–38.

Alexander, L. B. (1987). Unions: Social work. In A. Minahan (Ed.-in-chief), *Encyclopedia of social work* (18th ed., Vol. 2, pp. 793–800). Silver Spring, MD: National Association of Social Workers.

Berger, P. L., & Neuhaus, R. J. (1990). To empower people: The role of mediating structures in public policy. In D. L. Gies, J. S. Ott, & J. M. Shafritz (Eds.), *The nonprofit organization* (pp. 12–23). Pacific Grove, CA: Brooks/Cole.

Bradshaw, P., Murray, V., & Wolpin, J. (1992). Do nonprofit boards make a difference? An exploration of the relationships among board structure, process, and effectiveness. *Nonprofit and Voluntary Sector Quarterly, 21*(3), 227–249.

Bryson, J. M. (1988). *Strategic planning for public and nonprofit organizations.* San Francisco: Jossey-Bass.

deGrazia, A. (1957). *Grass roots in private welfare.* New York: New York University Press.

deTocqueville, A. (1961). *Democracy in America* (Vol. 11). New York: Schocken Books.

Filer, J. H. (1990). The Filer Commission Report (report of the Commission on Private Philanthropy and Public Needs). In D. L. Gies, J. S. Ott, & J. M. Shafritz (Eds.), *The nonprofit organization* (pp. 70–89). Pacific Grove, CA: Brooks/Cole.

Gaul, G. M., & Borowski, N. A. (1993, April 18–25). Warehouses of wealth: The tax-free economy. *The Philadelphia Inquirer*.

Gies, D. L., Ott, J. S., & Shafritz, J. (1990). Planning and policy formulation: Introduction. In *The nonprofit organization* (pp. 138–142). Pacific Grove, CA: Brooks/Cole.

Gummer, B. (1990). *The politics of social administration*. Englewood Cliffs, NJ: Prentice Hall.

Gurin, A. (1978). Conceptual and technical issues in the management of human services. In R. C. Sarri & Y. Hasenfeld (Eds.), *The management of human services* (pp. 289–308). New York: Columbia University Press.

Harvey, S. H., & Raider, M. C. (1984). Administrative burnout. *Administration in Social Work, 8*(2), 81–89.

Heimovics, R. D., & Herman, R. D. (1990). Responsibility for critical events in nonprofit organizations. *Nonprofit and Voluntary Sector Quarterly, 19*(1), 59–72.

Hodgkinson, V. A., & Weitzman, M. S. (1990). The independent sector: An overview. In D. L. Gies, J. S. Ott, & J. M. Shafritz (Eds.), *The nonprofit organization* (pp. 41–46). Pacific Grove, CA: Brooks/Cole.

Kramer, R. M. (1969). Ideology, status and power in board-executive relationships. In R. M. Kramer & H. Specht (Eds.), *Readings in community organization practice* (pp. 285–293). Englewood Cliffs, NJ: Prentice Hall.

Leiby, J. (1987). History of social welfare. In A. Minahan (Ed.-in-chief), *Encyclopedia of social work* (18th ed., Vol. 2, pp. 758–759). Silver Spring, MD: National Association of Social Workers.

Levy, C. (1979). The ethics of management. *Administration in Social Work, 3*, 277–288.

Macarov, D. (1991). *Certain change: Social work practice in the future*. Silver Spring, MD: National Association of Social Workers.

O'Neill, M. (1992). Ethical dimensions of nonprofit administration. *Nonprofit Management and Leadership, 3*(2), 199–213.

Perlmutter, F. D. (1971). Public funds and private agencies. *Child Welfare, 50*(3), 264–270.

Perlmutter, F. D. (1980). The Executive bind. In F. D. Perlmutter & S. Slavin (Eds.), *Leadership in social administration* (pp. 53–70). Philadelphia: Temple University Press.

Perlmutter, F. D. (1983). Caught in between: The middle management bind. *Administration in Social Work, 8*, 147–161.

Perlmutter, F. D. (1984). The professionalization of volunteer administration. In F. Schwartz (Ed.),*Voluntarism and social work practice: A growing collaboration* (pp. 117–127). Lanham, MD: University Press of America.

Perlmutter, F. D. (1988a). Administering alternative social programs. In L. Ginsberg & P. Keys (Eds.), *New management in human services* (pp. 167–183). Silver Spring, MD: National Association of Social Workers.

Perlmutter, F. D. (1988b). *Alternative social agencies: Administrative strategies.* New York: Haworth Press.

Perlmutter, F. D. (1990). *Changing hats: From social work practice to administration.* Washington, DC: National Association of Social Workers Press.

Perlmutter, F. D., & Adams, C. T. (1990). The voluntary sector and for-profit ventures: The transformation of American social welfare? *Administration in Social Work, 14*(1), 1–14.

Perlmutter, F. D., & Adams, C. T. (1994). Family service executives in a hostile environment: Managers or leaders? *Families in Society, 75*(7), 439–446.

Perlmutter, F. D., Adams, C. T., & Kramer, D. (1990, May). *The changing contract of American nonprofits.* Paper presented at the annual meeting of the Association of Voluntary Action Scholars, London.

Peters, T. J., & Waterman, R. J. (1983). *In search of excellence: Lessons from America's best run companies.* New York: Harper & Row.

Rose-Ackerman, S. (1990). Unfair competition and corporate income taxation In D. L. Gies, J. S. Ott, & J. M. Shafritz (Eds.), *The nonprofit organization* (pp. 91–108). Pacific Grove, CA: Brooks/Cole.

Scrivner, G. N. (1990). 100 years of tax policy changes affecting charitable organizations. In D. L. Gies, J. S. Ott, & J. M. Shafritz (Eds.), *The nonprofit organization* (pp. 126–137). Pacific Grove, CA: Brooks/Cole.

Stone, M. M. (1989). Planning as strategy in nonprofit organizations: An exploratory study. *Nonprofit and Voluntary Sector Quarterly, 18*(4), 297–315.

Wilensky, H., & Lebeaux, C. (1958). *Industrial society and social welfare.* New York: Russell Sage Foundation.

PART II
Cross-national Case Studies

CHAPTER THREE

Australia

Moving in from the Fringe

Mark Lyons, Julie Nyland, and Sallie Saunders

Elsie Women's Refuge and the Sydney Rape Crisis Centre were established by groups of feminists galvanized by the same event—a two-day conference, "Women Against the Violent Society," in Sydney in March 1974. Concern was focused on two major forms of violence against women: domestic violence and sexual assault. Both groups sought to change public attitudes and public policy while at the same time offering assistance and support to the women victims of domestic violence and rape. Each organization took up issues that had been suppressed or marginalized by mainstream social and political institutions and, in so doing, directly challenged many of those institutions.

At the time of their conception, Elsie Women's Refuge and the Sydney Rape Crisis Centre were very clearly fringe organizations. They were path-breaking groups, and the women involved regarded this work as an extension of their radical feminist commitment to social revolution. They perceived themselves as acting outside the existing structures and therefore began without thought of seeking financial support from the government. Each group chose to organize as a collective. This was a conscious choice, designed to challenge the power of the patriarchy by eschewing its preferred hierarchical and bureaucratic forms of organization. These collective structures were based on principles of equal responsibility, task sharing, and direct access to and equal participation in the decision-making process. The two collectives saw themselves as political organizations involved in a campaign to change fundamental values and structures of society—radical ideas and actions that placed them on the fringe of Australian society.

Today, Elsie Women's Refuge is one of almost 200 women's refuges throughout Australia that receive a total of $40 million in funding from

Commonwealth and state governments. It and similar organizations provide a refuge for women and their children escaping domestic violence. The Sydney Rape Crisis Centre receives grants from both the Commonwealth and the state governments to provide advocacy and support to women and children who have been sexually assaulted; it is the only nonprofit organization providing such services in New South Wales. There are, however, a large number of sexual assault services for adult and child victims of sexual assault provided by the state of New South Wales Department of Health through public hospitals.

During the past 18 years, Elsie Women's Refuge and the Sydney Rape Crisis Centre have moved in from the fringe. Each is entirely dependent on government grants for its revenue, and each has experienced significant changes in government policy toward domestic violence and sexual assault. These changes have addressed many of the concerns that initially motivated the women who established the two collectives. Finally, each collective has lost much of its original vision of a transformed world. Mostly, their members concern themselves with issues regarding the provision of services, management structures, and staffing issues. Although they maintain their feminist philosophy and a form of collective management, these groups are not greatly different from other nonprofit service providers.

The section that follows describes the achievements and the organizational transformation that have marked the path in from the fringe taken by these two organizations. First, however, it is necessary to provide a sketch of the changing Australian social and political environment in which they emerged and grew.

The Context

Australia's Political System

Australia has a federal system of government. The Australian constitution bestows on the national or Commonwealth government sole authority over some policy fields, such as defense, foreign affairs, and social security; in other policy fields, the Commonwealth government shares responsibility with six state and two territory governments. In many of these other policy fields, the Commonwealth government's involvement has little or no constitutional mandate but, nonetheless, the Commonwealth has attained considerable power by virtue of its dominant fiscal role. Thus, a pattern has emerged of fluctuating Commonwealth government initiative and innovation in the provision of human services.

Australian governments, state and national, are formed either by a Labor party or a by a Liberal or National party, most usually with the latter two in coalition. The Labor party was founded by the trade union movement in the 1890s and still has trade union links. This party tends to pursue more socially progressive policies than the Liberal or National parties, which still have strong links to the business and rural sectors. Labor tends to favor a stronger role for the Commonwealth government.

1970 to 1975: Years of Reform

Australia, as did other Western nations, enjoyed unprecedented prosperity during the 1950s and 1960s. For two decades, it was governed by a conservative Liberal/National party coalition. These 20 years of prosperity produced pressures for change that were becoming evident by the late 1960s. During the 1960s, there was a huge expansion in secondary and higher education. The postwar baby boom generation was better educated than any age group before it. Such education encouraged the questioning of existing institutions and practices. Many baby boomers became galvanized in the late 1960s by the movement against Australia's involvement in the Vietnam War and then went on to challenge and change social institutions and practices. A discourse on human rights emerged, inspired by examples from the United States and Europe. The state, big business, and the professions—along with social institutions such as marriage and religion—were denounced for the way in which they oppressed women, Aborigines, young people, and working people. Liberation and empowerment became the objective of the campaigning and organizing efforts of these reformers. The community was the locus of their organizing, and the collective and the commune the favored forms.

The Australian Labor party, in opposition nationally for 22 years, successfully played on the popular belief that it was time for a change and was elected to national government at the end of 1972. The new prime minister, Edward Gough Whitlam, began massively reforming government policies and institutions. His government generated many policy changes and opened government access to newly emerging groups and ideas.

But the Whitlam government lasted only three years. The pace and scope of its reforms generated resistance and hostility. More important, worldwide inflation—followed by the Organization of Petroleum Exporting Countries (OPEC) oil price increases—threw national economies into a slump; economic stagnation followed. In November 1975, the Whitlam government was dismissed, and a few weeks later, a newly elected Liberal/National party government set out to undo many of the Labor government's reforms.

Australia's Second Wave of Feminism

At the leading edge of the social upheaval of the 1960s and early 1970s was a rejuvenation of the "women's movement." Feminism had been an important catalyst for social change in Australia from the 1890s until

1914. Australia was one of the first countries to enfranchise women, but that first wave of feminism had been overwhelmed by complex and primarily conservative social forces shaped and energized by Australia's involvement in World War I. In the 1920s and 1930s, small groups of primarily educated middle-class women sustained the feminist cause, but this had little impact. Women were actively encouraged to enter the work force during World War II to replace men who had enlisted in the armed services. Employers were directed to pay male wages to those women who replaced men in the work force to discourage employers from retaining a cheaper work force at the end of the war and to underline the fact that women were simply "caretaking" the men's jobs. Although World War II gave women a far greater economic role, this was relinquished at the war's end. Feminism achieved little between 1940 and 1970.

However, in the early 1970s, inspired by overseas examples, the feminist movement (known then as "women's liberation") reemerged as a significant new social force. The movement encompassed a wide range of political stances—from moderate liberal feminism to newly emerging radical feminist critiques of male domination. Many saw the state as irredeemably patriarchal, but others, reflecting a long-established tradition in Australian social reform movements, thought it could be used to advantage, even won over. In early 1972, the Women's Electoral Lobby (WEL) was formed in Melbourne to confront candidates for the national election with feminist demands. Most members of WEL were university educated. Many were employed in responsible positions in government, the media, or professional practice. They used the media and the electoral process effectively and quickly expanded their numbers and influence (Ryan, 1990). Their demands focused on equality for women in employment and education, on reproductive rights, and on child care (Sawer, 1990).

WEL was successful in establishing an opening within the newly elected Whitlam government. Several active members of WEL were appointed to senior positions on Whitlam's staff or within some of the new policy commissions from which Whitlam sought ideas to transform society. These senior feminists appointed others to less senior positions. Such feminist bureaucrats came to be known as "femocrats." Within government, the femocrats sought to change existing policies and practices that discriminated against women and to introduce new programs that would benefit women.

These early feminist successes within the Whitlam government were not applauded by all feminists. Many feminists were scornful of what they saw as a deeply compromised strategy. The term "femocrat" had been coined derisively to attack those who were thought to have sold out to the patriarchy. Yet, despite these denunciations, the femocrats continued to see themselves as part of a wider feminist movement, and they maintained close ties with many of their more radical sisters.

The tension between the strategy of working through state institutions and that of seeking to transform state and society from without was a constant source of debate and conflict within the feminist movement during the next decade. Yet in the end, most feminists accepted government funding for their projects and sought social reform via legislative reform. In this they reflected and reproduced the core of the Australian radical tradition in which, beginning with the trade union movement in the 19th century, the state was available for capture and use as a vehicle for social and economic reform.

These arguments were just emerging in the early 1970s and were associated with disagreement over what should constitute the feminist agenda. Issues such as rape and domestic violence had not been part of the WEL agenda in 1972. By 1974, however, the hidden existence of widespread male violence toward women was becoming central to the political concerns of many feminists. In this they were motivated by their knowledge of actual experiences of women and also by actions in other countries, most notably the example of Chiswick Women's Aid in Great Britain. Highlighting the issue of male violence became the work of feminists who advocated a more direct form of political action than that followed by WEL. They focused on the activities and behavior of men, rather than on the activities and behavior of government (McGregor & Hopkins, 1991). Within the women's movement itself, these feminists became the radical fringe.

It was these feminists who organized the Commission on Women and Violence in Sydney in March 1974, and it was from among this group that the two collectives that formed to create Elsie Women's Refuge and the Sydney Rape Crisis Centre drew their members.

Growth and Change in Government Support

An initial Commonwealth government grant was made to Elsie Women's Refuge in early 1975. It was the product of work by feminists within the bureaucracy and by those at Elsie who had lobbied ministers and generated considerable publicity. The grant came from the Community Health Program, a new initiative staffed by reformers who were more open to appeals from projects like Elsie than were those staff members administering the existing program for homeless people. The initial grant led to pressure from the other shelters that had formed quickly, modeled on Elsie's example. In June 1975, the government announced funding for 11 refuges throughout Australia. The Sydney Rape Crisis Centre was also funded from this allocation.

These actions created a momentum that assured continued growth in Commonwealth funding for women's refuges for two more years, despite the election of a conservative Liberal/National party government in December 1975. However, the determination of that government to curb Commonwealth involvement in human services provision soon became evident. Commonwealth support for the Community Health Program, which funded women's refuges, was reduced beginning in 1977; it ended in 1981. This forced women's shelters to rely increasingly on state governments for their survival and growth. Some state governments were supportive.

In 1976, a Labor government, led by Neville Wran, had been elected in the state of New South Wales (NSW). One of the first actions of the Wran government was to appoint a Women's Coordination Unit (WCU) reporting directly to Premier Wran, who generally was sympathetic to women's issues. An influential Women's Advisory Council (WAC) also was established to work closely with WCU. WCU enabled representatives from various feminist groups to have an active voice in policy development.

Like Whitlam, Wran was a lawyer, but unlike Whitlam, he was not inclined to attack inequality and injustice through new programs for social expenditure. He preferred legislative change, and his government, responding to the promptings of WCU, introduced important antidiscrimination and equal employment legislation, as well as significant amendments to laws covering domestic violence and sexual assault (NSW Women's Advisory Council, 1987). In 1977, WCU persuaded the NSW government to establish a task force to examine the treatment and care of victims of sexual offenses in NSW. Wran was keenly aware that the issue concerned not only feminists but also the medical and legal professions. It required a response that would avoid antagonizing these powerful groups. Membership on the task force was confined to senior public officials, most of whom were men.

In February 1978, after three months of meetings, the task force advised that rape and other sexual offenses be regarded as psychological–medical emergencies in which the care of the victim is of paramount importance. The task force recommended the establishment of specialist units in major public hospitals, an approach pioneered in several other states. The recommendations were adopted, and beginning in 1978 the state health system took responsibility for both the treatment and counseling of victims of sexual offenses and for the development of expertise in the area of sexual assault. Other recommendations for changes in the way the judicial system handled sexual assault required legislative change, which eventually occurred in 1981.

In 1981, WCU persuaded the government to establish another task force to investigate and recommend appropriate policy on domestic violence. Refuge workers had substantial representation on the task force, which strongly endorsed the role of women's refuges in addition to recommending other important changes to legislation and policy procedures. Shelter workers also were well represented on the Domestic Violence Monitoring Committee, established by the state government two years later.

The 1981 abolition of the Community Health Program and its threatened extinction of Commonwealth support for refuges spurred women's organizations around Australia to action. Later that year, thousands of women from all over Australia attended a major rally in the city of Canberra. A number of them stormed and occupied part of Parliament House, but the action had little impact on the government.

The Labor opposition proved more amenable to the women's cause. In March 1983, the Labor party, now led by Bob Hawke, was again elected to government at the Commonwealth level, and it immediately announced a $4 million commitment to support and expand women's shelters. The decline in Commonwealth government support for women's refuges had been reversed.

Meanwhile, bureaucratic activity was fashioning a more coherent policy for all forms of homelessness. Two programs were created effective January 1, 1985. One was the Crisis Accommodation Programme (CAP), which would provide capital funds for the purchase of emergency accommodation and would be administered by Commonwealth and state housing authorities; the other was the Supported Accommodation Assistance Programme (SAAP), which would provide recurrent funds for women's, youth, and general-use refuges through three separate subprograms. Both CAP and SAAP were to be funded jointly by Commonwealth and state governments but administered by the states. With minor changes, these two programs remain the means by which government support is provided to women's refuges today.

The creation of the SAAP program had two consequences. It provided a more settled funding base that gave a greater security to refuges, but it also accelerated the growth of state government bureaucracy—albeit initially largely feminist bureaucracies—to administer it. During the second half of the 1980s, refuges were required to submit an increasing number of forms and to abide by increasingly detailed rules. Initially, there was a determined resistance by women's refuges to many of these accountability and data collection procedures. Although feminist shelters resented this growing bureaucracy, its existence attested to their success. The model for providing assistance to victims of domestic violence, pioneered by Elsie, had become a major principle of government policy.

Meanwhile, the Sydney Rape Crisis Centre continued to receive government support. However, the community-based model for supporting victims of sexual assault that it pioneered was not more widely adopted; the reason for this is explored below. Although the center remained unique in NSW, it too experienced an increase in bureaucratic scrutiny.

Bureaucratic scrutiny soon escalated to pressure to conform to particular types of organization. In state elections in 1988, the Labor government in NSW was replaced by a Liberal/National party coalition government that was determined to introduce modern business management into the government bureaucracy. Within the state government bureaucracy, feminists either adapted to the new government's priorities or left. Pressure was increased on women's refuges and other feminist organizations to legally incorporate and adopt conventional models of governance and management. This meant abandoning the worker–collective form of management that many shelters followed and incorporating as associations. Several refuges were forced by threat of funding cuts to restructure. Others moved slowly to comply. Paradoxically, trade union initiatives at that time added pressure toward the same end.

One consequence of the long and powerful influence of the trade union movement on Australia's political and legal institutions is the existence of a comprehensive legal system covering industrial relations. Almost all aspects of workplace relations are covered by law and open to scrutiny by a special legal–industrial judiciary. In most industries and occupations, industrial awards (or legal judgments) determine rates of pay and other working conditions. These apply even if no employee in a firm or industry belongs to a union. Small, marginal, and newly emerging occupations and industries often begin without the cover of industrial awards, but as they grow, they attract union attention and come under the award-setting process.

For their first 15 years, women's shelters were not covered by industrial awards. In 1991, an industrial award for these areas was established. This award effectively removed from all refuges control over wage setting, but for collectives it also meant relinquishing their right to establish their own working conditions and added pressure to abandon the collective form of governance.

The Organizations

Elsie Women's Refuge

Galvanized by the intense and often painful testimony of women at the 1974 Commission on Women and Violence, a group of women took over two derelict houses on a housing estate owned by the Anglican Church. They opened the door of Australia's first refuge for women escaping male violence, and they named the shelter "Elsie" after the nameplate on one of the houses.

This action took place in March 1974 and received a great deal of publicity. It was quickly followed by similar actions elsewhere in the nation, and by the end of the year 10 other refuges had been established. Although the first few refuges were clearly and avowedly feminist, other shelters were quickly established by other groups, including church organizations.

Elsie and other feminist refuges were extremely articulate about their feminist aims. First, they wished to "create a point of contact between the Women's Movement and women in acute, desperate, and dangerous situations" (Women's Liberation Halfway House Collective, 1976, p. 37). The primary objectives of this point of contact were to

- enable a sharing of resources and information aimed at assisting these women—in a manner that promoted independence and self-determination. Refuges were quite clear about their intention to make women aware of the nature of oppression and to work against conventional notions of women's roles.

- create public awareness of the effects of women's oppression and of the need for social change.

- achieve these goals within a form of organization that would promote equality, participation, and "empowerment." The collective form was seen as a way of having "the means reflect the end." (Flaskas & Hounslow, 1980, p. 13)

Feminist refuges adamantly focused on the root cause of women's homelessness, the need for social change, their opposition to the "charity model," and their commitment to alleviating women's distress within a new model of service.

This philosophy was reinforced by such public statements of objective as wanting "to make people aware of the [necessary] revolutionary change in society" and "to expose the fact that despite some monetary support, the practice of the government is not to radically change the situation of women but rather to temporarily alleviate their situation" (Women's Liberation Halfway House Collective, 1976, p. 37).

The initial phase for Elsie, as well as for other refuges, was one of intense activity and reliance on sympathetic publicity to generate donations to keep the refuge operating. Elsie was entirely operated by women volunteers who took turns staffing the shelter on a roster system. The refuge offered women and their children meals, information, a place to sleep, and assistance with working out their situation.

The women organized as a collective—a symbol of their antipatriarchal philosophy. The notion of collectivity also incorporated the service users.

As part of attempting to enable women to regain power over their own lives, service users were entitled to belong to the collective and were encouraged to see the refuge workers as resources rather than "social workers."

Elsie operated for nine months as a totally volunteer operation. It maintained a large corps of women who undertook roster duty and managed the organization. The refuge was inundated with women seeking assistance immediately after its opening—many of these women had been in situations of extreme violence for more than 20 years. The majority of women came directly from their homes, but a few were homeless women who did not want to return to the charitable shelters or pyschiatric hospitals. Unfortunately, the two houses were in a state of severe disrepair, and the living conditions were overcrowded. Laundry and kitchen facilities were inadequate, and the backyard was periodically awash with sewage.

These conditions, and the severity of the women's situations, made for extremely demanding work. Early in its history, the organization realized that sustaining the refuge solely on volunteer labor and donated material was not feasible and that government funding was necessary. Within the immediate collective, there was very little dissension over this decision. The visibly appalling physical conditions and the sensational nature of many of the women's stories of violence created a wave of public sympathy that, in turn, placed great pressure on government to respond.

In January 1975, Elsie received its first government funding from the Commonwealth government. This was given as a "once only" payment without commitment to ongoing support. This payment enabled the refuge to employ its first paid worker.

In July 1975, after much lobbying by feminists around the country, the Commonwealth government agreed to fund all 11 existing refuges. This second funding was sufficient for Elsie to take on six paid workers, with some expectation of ongoing government support. The organization continued to operate as a collective, formed by paid staff and unpaid (volunteer) collective members. Some unpaid collective members continued to carry out roster duties, but this diminished over the following year.

The first paid staff positions had designated roles, which in theory denoted areas of specialization such as drug dependency counselor, bookkeeper, and child support worker. In practice, much of the work was approached without specialization, and everyone was paid the same wage.

The first few years of Elsie's existence were volatile. In addition to the difficult working conditions, the organization was also "finding its feet" with regard to its operation. This involved the collective refining its mission, sorting out the mechanisms of managing "collectively," developing operational policies, and negotiating its internal and external political environment.

The organization's relationships with external agencies were varied and predominantly tense. Government authorities and other agencies found it difficult to deal with an organization that had no "boss," and in which even minor decisions had to be referred to the collective.

Elsie also found itself under attack from local residents, with a hostile campaign being waged for almost a year. An arson attempt on the refuge was made late in 1975, followed by anonymous threats and vitriolic articles in the local newspaper. The hostility was focused on the feminist politics of the organization and used stereotyped images of lesbians as its attack point.

At the organizational level, Elsie was going through the transformation from volunteer staffing to paid staffing. By early 1976, tensions were evident between paid staff and unpaid collective members, with disputes arising over levels of direct contact with the refuge work. Underlying some of these disputes were differing viewpoints on unpaid work in general and an antivoluntarist stance by some collective members.

These political disagreements began to extend to "ex-residents"— women who had used the service and remained in contact with the shelter. By mid-1976, a number of ex-residents were taking an active (albeit unpaid) role in the refuge.

After a series of debates around these issues and the resignations of some collective members, a radical restructuring took place. A number of unpaid, ex-resident collective members became paid staff; this change was enabled by dividing existing wages among all of the members. This "collectivization" of wages created a "worker collective" (with no external or nonworker members and reduced wages for some of the paid staff). Job differentiation was abandoned, and a policy of task rotation was adopted.

By late 1976, the refuge had cemented its operational form as a worker collective, and the organizational structure did not change until the early 1990s. By 1979, growing problems with Commonwealth funding and a concern about the influence of strong conservative "non-feminist" refuges brought feminist shelters together. A state conference was held for NSW refuges, and the NSW Women's Refuge Movement was born. Although alliances among feminist refuges had been strong, this was the first formal process for combined action.

The movement proved to be a strong and powerful force. It undoubtedly provided protection for individual services and enhanced the general bargaining position of the refuges with government. As a member of the alliance, Elsie was surrounded by like-minded organizations and was viewed as central to this political force. This group in turn linked with feminist refuges nationwide and became an effective national lobbying force. With the routinization of refuge funding under the 1985 SAAP program and the resultant increased bureaucratic scrutiny, there has been a slow but significant change in Elsie and in the refuge movement generally.

External pressures over the past few years have combined to force Elsie to review its operations in staffing, legal status, and administration. In 1991, after direct intervention by government officials concerned about irregular management practices, a virtual total change of collective membership occurred. The new staff set about "tidying up" the systems. The organization also formalized its operation by incorporating as an association, and in so doing, reintroduced an external collective—or management committee—of nonworker collective members. Initially, the external collective is unlikely to operate as more than a formality, approving decisions taken by the worker collective, but this move represents conformance with the more traditional management committee structure.

Over the 18 years of Elsie's operation, its goals have not changed, but, in practice, provision of service is now the primary focus. Workers see their involvement in community education and action as important but limited by lack of time and energy. There is a tendency to perceive the refuge as less radical than in its legendary early days of turbulence.

Sydney Rape Crisis Centre

Like Elsie Women's Refuge, the Sydney Rape Crisis Centre was opened in 1974 by a group of women who felt compelled to respond to the issues raised at the Commission on Women and Violence earlier that year. These women were feminists—many of whom had been raped—and their message to the women of Sydney was both terse and provocative:

TO ALL WOMEN

Any man (stranger, father, brother, husband, pack of men or policeman) can rape (any forced sexual encounter) any female (you) using any weapon (including blackmail, numbers, mateship, brute strength, status, or the concept that "men are aggressive and women are passive") anywhere (including your own home) at any time. A Rape Crisis Centre opened in Sydney today at Women's House. (Sydney Rape Crisis Centre, 1974, p.7)

The Sydney Rape Crisis Centre also published its three main aims:

1. to provide support and help to women who have been raped—including women who have been raped in the past and are still living with the memory

2. to change the law in those respects in which it discriminates against the victim

3. to act against rape, especially to change community attitudes toward this crime and, particularly, toward its victims. (Sydney Rape Crisis Centre, 1974, p. 7)

The center set a decidedly feminist double agenda that aimed to improve the lives of women *and* change the fundamental values and structures of society.

The center not only supported women through any required medical and legal procedures, but it facilitated their long-term recovery by encouraging them to share their experiences and examine their feelings of shame, guilt, and self-condemnation within a feminist analytical framework. Early members of the organization saw this method of hearing women out of silence as fundamentally political work that was integral to the other support services.

The Sydney Rape Crisis Centre operated entirely on a voluntary basis for the first 12 months. A large group of 20 to 30 women volunteered their labor and skills to offer 24-hour, seven-days-per-week crisis telephone counseling and ongoing support for women who had been raped. The group also provided an emergency rescue service, a media watch, and an information and referral service, and they organized support groups, discussion groups, and self-defense classes. Motivated by anger and sustained by the collective, many of the women pursued a wider political agenda. Collective members undertook a punishing schedule of consciousness-raising activities, action committees, publicity campaigns, and speaking engagements with other community groups and students.

The work of this early period also included the development of a collective organizational structure. As feminists, the women who established the Sydney Rape Crisis Centre were critical of hierarchical structures that reproduced existing power relations, legitimized domination, and silenced resistance. They created an organizational structure that sought to avoid these problems and that reflected the center's commitment to decision making by consensus, structured skill-sharing, and job rotation. Giving women access to the power of decision making and the responsibility to be competent within the experiential learning framework of the collective were the organizational "means to the end" of women taking control over their lives.

At first most women participated in all the tasks of the center, but for some collective members the constant reliving of their experiences, through counseling other women who had been raped, became overwhelming. Tasks were reallocated so that women could be relieved from answering the telephones and thus, by the end of the first year, a division of labor was established even though positions were not formally defined.

During the same period, another important debate took place within the collective. For some women, the concept of seeking government funding for their work seemed ludicrous. One early collective member described it as equivalent to expecting the government to fund a group opposing the Vietnam War. Other collective members were totally against being accountable to the patriarchal state and regarded the issue as dangerous to their radical feminist mission. The opposing view was put forth by another group who saw great irony in "getting the government to pay for the revolution."

In 1975, the Sydney Rape Crisis Centre received its first grant from the Commonwealth government, and a number of collective members resigned in protest. As a result of this volatile debate, the remaining collective members were very aware of the dangers of selling out to the patriarchal state and resolved to remain revolutionary. This resolution was evident in their political activities. One memorable campaign used the slogan "Dead men don't rape" and sparked a shocked reaction from many community members, including other feminists.

With funding came the inevitable conflict between paid and unpaid workers. The funding was not adequate for a 24-hour service, and many committed women remained as unpaid collective members and covered the rosters with the small group of paid workers. Lengthy discussions were held to modify or develop policies, procedures, and systems that took account of the changed relationships within the collective structure. Despite this effort, some tensions remained, and lengthy discussions at weekly collective meetings became part of the normal routine.

By 1977, the work of the center had increased markedly, and the debate over funding was heading for resolution. Most members of the collective agreed that the state must accept its responsibilities by providing adequate funding for their services, and they campaigned vigorously toward this end as they continued their consciousness-raising activities.

At this time the nature of the political campaigning by its staff marked the Sydney Rape Crisis Centre as a radical organization determined to challenge the establishment and to get the issue of rape onto the political agenda. Although the creation of the Sexual Assault Task Force by the NSW government in November 1977 demonstrated a measure of success in this effort, the center's omission from membership on the task force meant that it was not able to control or influence the task force's agenda. In addition, the center was unable to use that forum to demonstrate its expertise and establish the validity of its alternative organization as a model for assisting the victims of sexual assault.

However, one such opportunity was granted when the Sydney Rape Crisis Centre representatives were invited to a seminar held by the task force before presentation of its report. At that seminar, the representatives vigorously opposed the proposed recommendations for hospital-based services, claiming that hospitals would institutionalize the care of victims of sexual offenses. They argued for the establishment of more community-based women's health centers that could incorporate specialized and holistic sexual assault services.

Despite the fact that this may have been more cost effective (and possibly more appropriate), it was not an established alternative, and no hard evidence was available to support the argument. Even apart from that deficiency, the views of the Sydney Rape Crisis Centre may not have been given serious consideration by the task force. The task force report described the Sydney Rape Crisis Centre as an organization whose workers were young, untrained, and unlikely to stay more than six months because of low wages (Inter-Departmental Task Force, 1978). Given this view and the interests of the medico-legal establishment, the task force was unlikely to be swayed from recommending the professional approach of a specialist hospital unit.

Following the report of the task force and acceptance of its recommendations by the state government, the Sydney Rape Crisis Centre was effectively isolated as the only community-based feminist service for female victims of sexual assault. The report's calls for extra funds were ignored as the state government diverted resources to the hospital-based centers and made political capital out of its impressive responses to the needs of victims of sexual offenses.

Tensions within the collective were exacerbated during this difficult period and, by the following year, had reached a crisis point. Many of the unpaid collective members urged the collective to adopt a more moderate and less confrontational approach in public campaigns to increase community support and, therefore, the possibility of being granted extra funds. Other members (mostly the paid workers) were convinced that all of the work of the Sydney Rape Crisis Centre must reflect its radical feminist analysis, and they refused to tame their activities. The debates over this issue led to a major collective split, and by 1980, collective membership was restricted to paid workers of the organization.

The new collective withdrew to reconsider its role and methods of operation. Without volunteers, the paid workers had to cover all the tasks of the organization, and new workers had to be chosen carefully to ensure that they could do so. An emerging concern to ensure that women from groups discriminated against in the wider society—such as aboriginal women and women from non-English-speaking backgrounds—were granted equal opportunities for employment added an additional set of dilemmas. The development of an employment policy consumed a great deal of time and effort. Nevertheless, the basic form of a worker collective remained in place for a decade.

The restriction on collective membership and the marginalization of the service (by the development of outside hospital-based services) served to increase the isolation of the Sydney Rape Crisis Centre. To some extent, the organization counteracted this by meeting with other women's services in discussion groups to plan and carry out political actions across the state. The center also joined the Women's Health, Information, Resources and Crisis Centres Association, which was formed in 1981 to lobby on behalf of women's services and was active in the 1981 campaigns to "defend and extend women's services" and in 1984 an unsuccessful campaign to get a national women's services program funded by the Commonwealth government. These activities kept the Sydney Rape Crisis Centre involved with women's services across the state and responsive to the other issues being debated by various groups.

The passage of time saw the Sydney Rape Crisis Centre collective modify its hostility toward the government. In 1981 the NSW parliament enacted major changes in sexual assault legislation. The center led a campaign arguing that the impact of the legislation needed to be monitored. In 1983 the government agreed and established a monitoring committee. One of its members was from the Sydney Rape Crisis Centre.

By the early 1990s, the Sydney Rape Crisis Centre collective was becoming increasingly fearful that the state government might use the Centre's atypical collective structure and lack of formal legal identity as an excuse to withdraw funding. A new industrial award also appeared to require certain changes to the collective's governance. A comprehensive review was initiated, resulting in a number of significant changes. The center was incorporated as an association, although it still bent the rules of the Association's Incorporations Act to retain some link with its more radical past. A management committee has been established with some nonworker members who have exclusive responsibility for employment-related decisions. The internal shape of the collective also has changed with the appointment of a coordinator and an administrative worker and with the adoption of detailed job descriptions that clearly define the tasks of each worker. The practices of the organization are now clearly focused on the provision of services. The old days of involvement in turbulent political action are recorded in extensive media files, but the files have not been added to since 1988.

Similarities and Differences

Both Elsie Women's Refuge and the Sydney Rape Crisis Centre were set up in 1974 under similar circumstances with distinct similarities in their goals, vision, and political philosophies. Both organizations developed within the same political and social context, and it is clear from their histories that although diverging in some respects, they have essentially changed in similar ways.

Mission and Ideology

Both organizations were formed to challenge social relations and societal attitudes prevalent at the time. They had in common a radical feminist philosophy, which led them to perceive themselves as having a revolutionary, rather than reformist, mission. Each was focused on social issues that Australian culture of the 1970s did not recognize. They directly challenged the social myths and the pattern of social relations that those myths sustained—particularly relations between women and men.

The original missions of both organizations were consciously aimed at changing both societal attitudes toward domestic violence and sexual assault and the social structures that supported the very existence of these crimes. At a practical level, social policy and legislation became the foci of concern. This movement occurred sooner for Elsie than for the Sydney Rape Crisis Centre. In the latter, the debate over whether to accept government support was more intense, and confrontationist tactics were maintained for a longer period of time. But within a decade, members of the Sydney Rape Crisis Centre, as with those of Elsie before them, were sitting on government committees. Both organizations set out to offer direct assistance to victims of male violence. In approaching this service element, these organizations also consciously challenged prevailing philosophies of the helping professions—a major component of their mission was to offer assistance in a way that empowered the service user. Now, nearly two decades later, it is clear that although their formal goals have not changed, members of both organizations are primarily preoccupied with the work of providing support services to women victims of male violence.

Governance

Elsie Women's Refuge and the Sydney Rape Crisis Centre were established as collectives, and this structure in itself marked them as "alternative organizations." For feminist organizations the vesting of authority in the group rather than in the individual is central; all members of the collective must share equally in the management of the organization.

Initially both organizations relied entirely on volunteer effort. Later, with government financial support, both organizations were able to employ staff. This, in turn, led to significant debates about the role of paid and unpaid workers in the collective. Both groups eventually resolved to become worker collectives, although that decision was more difficult for the Sydney Rape Crisis Centre.

Both organizations institutionalized an egalitarian structure, minimized job differentiation, used consensus decision making, and employed staff more on the basis of life experience and homogeneity of political values than on formal qualifications or specialized skills. For both organizations the collective mode of operation initially was experimental, and a constant dialogue was carried on about its mechanics as the women discovered that all was not necessarily easy or equal in a collective organization.

Collectives are marked by decision-making practices that involve fulsome discussion, openly based on principles or values and appealing to ethics rather than to rules or precedents. Decisions are made by consensus rather than by voting. In the cases of Elsie and the Sydney Rape Crisis Centre, all decision making was deferred to a weekly collective meeting. Both within and outside these meetings, discussion was constant about the appropriate political response to internal problems and to problems imposed by the external environment. These political considerations were integrated into collective functioning, along with such practical issues as grocery shopping and attending to individual women's needs.

This mode of operation fostered a reactive form of organizational policy-making, with most policy decisions being made by the collectives in response to existing problems. The organizations began with a few simple house rules and procedures for responding to situations but quickly developed a complex set of policies arising out of the organization's actual day-to-day experiences. The collective form of organizations stands in sharp contrast to bureaucratic forms. To bureaucrats who were not sympathetic to the collective cause, collectives, with their time-consuming decision-making processes, seemed inefficient. Worker collectives seemed also to lack accountability. In the mid-1980s, growing emphasis from government on better management began to put pressure on all government-funded organizations. Since a change of state government in 1988, intense scrutiny of the administrative operations of many funded organizations convinced those organizations to review or overhaul their administration.

Elsie and the Sydney Rape Crisis Centre have both responded to this pressure by increasing the formality of their operation, incorporating and establishing a separate governing body, although it is one that operates along collective lines. In response to this pressure and also to pressure from the trade unions, employee relations have also become more formalized. There is also a suggestion that greater formality was sought by the members of both collectives. Members were from a younger generation of feminists than the founders of the two organizations, and they were more pragmatic and goal-oriented. Some of the features of collective organization seemed to them unnecessarily cumbersome.

The end result has been that both organizations have taken on facets of a bureaucratic structure while retaining essential elements of collectivity. They are now a form of hybrid organization of the kind discussed by Bordt (1990) in her article on feminist collectives in the United States.

Relations with Government

It has been in their relations with government that the greatest divergence between the two organizations has occurred. Essentially, the Sydney Rape Crisis Centre was more hostile to government and, as a consequence, has less influence on government policy. The reasons for this difference are worth exploring.

The question of seeking or accepting government funding was an important issue for feminist organizations in the mid-1970s. On one side of the debate were arguments that government funding was essential if such services were to continue and that the state should be forced to accept responsibility for such services. Inherent in the argument for government funding was an element of hostility toward volunteers. On the other side, there were arguments that an acceptance of government funding would constrain political activity and weaken the organization's capacity to bring about social change. There were accusations that such organizations would simply "prop up" existing social inequalities and would fast become part of the "welfare furniture" (McFerran, 1990, p. 201). The dilemma was posed in late 1975 by members of the Melbourne refuge:

> Whether we can threaten the relations of power and control that form the basis of this society while being financed by the system that maintains them and how far we can use government funding to develop the potential of the Halfway House as a political weapon are the most important questions. " (Women's Liberation Halfway House Collective, 1980, p. 3).

Within Elsie, the debate was soon over. The condition of its accommodations and the pressing needs of its residents quickly convinced the collective that financial support was needed. Their view was that the work they were doing was properly the responsibility of the state. This made it clear that the source of that support had to be the government. The debate within the Sydney Rape Crisis Centre collective was longer, and its resolution to accept government aid led to a determination to shun any other form of compromise with the state.

The Sydney Rape Crisis Centre's more radical stance against the state helps explain why, when the NSW government established task forces on sexual assault and domestic violence, workers from Elsie were closely involved with the latter task force, whereas the Sydney Rape

Crisis Centre was excluded from the former task force. But this explanation is only part of the story. The wider configuration of interests and practices that formed around these two issues was very different.

Elsie's model for addressing the problem of domestic violence quickly generated many imitations. Although the Elsie collective saw its provision of a refuge as only part of its project, that part seemed to many, including traditional welfare organizations and conservative bureaucrats, to be an "obvious" solution to a problem. Generally, it was not difficult for the femocrats to win widespread endorsement within government for the refuge model. By contrast, there were already two powerful groups with vested interests in sexual assault—the medical and the legal professions. In addition, several states already had moved to establish sexual assault centers within public hospitals. Even if the Sydney Rape Crisis Centre collective had not been so hostile to the state, it is unlikely that the center's model of support for the victims of sexual assault would have become government policy. Nonetheless, despite its hostility to government policy, the Sydney Rape Crisis Centre continued to receive financial support, protected by the femocrats and its pioneering reputation. Over time, the center moderated its position.

The passage of time has seen a convergence in the attitude of the two organizations toward the government. By the end of the 1980s, they both faced a suspicious government determined to require the organizations it funded to conform to a single governance model. This and other pressures led both organizations to incorporate and to modify their governance accordingly.

Conclusion

Elsie Women's Refuge and the Sydney Rape Crisis Centre both began as fringe organizations, but in the almost 20 years since their formation, they have moved in from the edge of society. They began with two broad goals: Each sought the elimination of male violence toward women by radical social change; to this end, each pursued radical confrontationist activities. But each also sought to provide immediate practical assistance to women who had suffered male violence.

It was their confrontational campaigning that did much to place these organizations on the fringe of society. It also placed them at odds with other feminists who were seeking social change by working from within government. Yet they were soon successful in placing their issues on the public agenda. This in turn enabled the femocrats to win appropriate policy and legislative changes.

These changes were achieved within a decade. Violence by men against women has not diminished, but its existence now is recognized and generally deplored. There are policies and programs that address the problem, and although these are far from perfect, their existence makes it difficult to sustain the campaigning motivation that initially galvanized the two organizations back in 1974.

There is, however, a continuing need for the services these organizations provide, and it is to this end that most of their energy is now directed. Their activities continue to be informed by feminist analysis, but both organizations are largely unremarkable components of government programs. As the service-providing goal has come to predominate, largely in response to external forces, the worker–collective form of organization that each group had adopted in the early years has been modified.

Elsie Women's Refuge and the Sydney Rape Crisis Centre were important pioneering elements of the feminist movement in the 1970s. Part of the success of the movement was to obtain public recognition of the existence of violence against women and to create government programs to address the problem. The violence continues and the programs are far from perfect, but the existence of these programs and the participation of Elsie and the Sydney Rape Crisis Centre in them are testimony to the success of the organizations and to their movement in from the fringe.

References

Bordt, R. (1990). *How alternative ideas become institutions: The case of feminist collectives*. PONPO Working Paper 159/ISPS. Working Paper 2159. New Haven, CT: Yale University.

Flaskas, C., & Hounslow, B. (1980, September). Government intervention and right wing attacks on feminist services. *Scarlet Woman*, *11*, 13–21.

Inter-Departmental Task Force. (1978). *Care for victims of sexual offenses*. Sydney, Australia: Government Printer.

McFerran, L. (1990). Interpretation of a frontline state: Australian women's refuges and the state. In S. Watson (Ed.), *Playing the state*. Sydney, Australia: Allen & Unwin.

McGregor, H., & Hopkins, A. (1991). *Working for change: The movement against domestic violence*. Sydney, Australia: Allen & Unwin.

NSW Women's Advisory Council. (1987). *A decade of change: Women in NSW 1976–1986. Sydney, Australia: NSW Women's Coordination Unit.

Ryan, L. (1990). Feminism and the federal bureaucracy. In S. Watson (Ed.), *Playing the state* (pp. 71–84). Sydney, Australia: Allen & Unwin.

Sawer, M. (1990). *Sisters in suits: Women and public policy in Australia.* Sydney, Australia: Allen & Unwin.

Sydney Rape Crisis Centre. (1974). Views on rape. *Womanspeak, 1*(1), 7.

Women's Liberation Halfway House Collective. (1976). *Herstory of Halfway House.* Melbourne, Australia: Author.

Women's Liberation Halfway House Collective. (1980, September). Halfway house: Collective work is a political act. *Scarlet Woman, 11,* 3.

CHAPTER FOUR

Croatia

The Women's Alliance

Arpad Barath and Ljiljana Bastaic-Barath

Women's voluntary action in Croatia has one of the oldest grassroots historical traditions in Central Europe. In the medieval cities of Dalmatia, such as Dubrovnik and Split, women had a highly respected social status and more important, an egalitarian "ownership" with men in marital, economic, educational, and moral matters. Thus, in a Renaissance document, it is noted that "once the marriage is set, the husband is not the [sole] owner of his own body but the wife has it, and the wife is not the sole owner of her own body but the husband has it" (Kotruljevic, 1458/ 1573/1989 p. 431).

The traditional code of equity between genders was an integral part of Croatian peasant culture as well, valid until recent times (Erlich, 1978). In the peasant family

> *The wife is not a slave; rather she is the respected caretaker of the family. As soon as she comes to live under the husband's roof, she obtains all the economic and social rights equally shared among all the other members of her new home. Women obtain all their rights and ownership in the household through legal marriage and not by means of any formal inventory of possessions as claimed by our public law.* (Ivsic, 1936, pp. 58–59)

The case study that is the focus of this chapter is of the Women's Alliance of Croatia (WAC). It is important to explain that while the breakdown of the former country of Yugoslavia is still in process and the brutality of war a present reality, the nation state of Croatia has been formed, and this is the national context of this discussion. However, the historical background can be presented only from within the broader context of the territories that composed the former Yugoslavia. Reference will be made both to "the former Yugoslavia" as well as to "the territories" that were included in the formation of Yugoslavia but that existed prior to the formation of that country in 1943.

This chapter discusses the WAC with a focus on its historical context. Three distinct phases are identified: (1) the origins of the women's self-empowerment movement from the latter part of the 19th century to presocialist Yugoslavia, 1918 to 1941; (2) the socialist women's movement in Marshal Tito's Yugoslavia (1941 to 1990); and (3) the reemergence of women's voluntary action in the present independent Republic of Croatia in the 1990s. This historical perspective is essential for an understanding of the current realities in Croatia that affect the WAC.

Women's Activity in the Presocialist Era: 1870s to 1941

With the rise of civic and urban society in the former Yugoslavia during the second half of the 19th century, women's voluntary activism became a much-praised status symbol among wealthier and more-educated women. The first formal women's voluntary organization, the Association of Working Women, was organized in Zagreb in 1874. This first Croatian model organization emerged in the same decade as the first formal social action organization of women in Europe, established in Germany in 1865 by Luisa Otto-Peters. Between 1884 and 1901, additional women's organizations were established in Rijeka, Zadar, and Ljubljana (Kecman, 1978). All of these groups included men, although often they were in separate sections of the organization. All of the organizations had political and social action agendas.

In the first decade of this century, women's action groups and programs began to mushroom throughout the territories. Important to this process was the groups' growing access to the mass media. For example, during 1908, Zagreb's political magazine, *Slobodna rijec (Free Word)*, issued a call for papers concerning women's issues. In 1914, the first women's union was organized, consisting largely of female workers employed in the trade industry. Similar initiatives of women's social activism continuously emerged throughout the territories that eventually, in 1918, became the Kingdom of Serbs, Croats, and Slovens and then later Yugoslavia.

During World War I and after, women in the former Yugoslavia, along with those in other countries, became emancipated. Women sought employment in growing numbers and began attending schools and universities. Civic organizations for women were established, usually by wealthy or educated women who were motivated by such social/humanitarian concerns as the problems of people with disabilities and youth and women's political rights. Through the offering of courses, seminars, and public lectures to the general public, these organizations created a great impact among the poor, who otherwise could not afford any training or education. This first decade of the 20th century saw the flourishing of such organizations as the Association of Yugoslav Women, the Feminist Alliance, and the Association of Working Women and Girls—all of which had distinct social, educational, and political agendas (Kecman, 1978).

Women's Activity in Socialist Yugoslavia: 1945 to 1990

With the outbreak of World War II, a new chapter in the dynamics of women's voluntary action began. Tito's "People's Liberation War" led to the reconstruction of the territories into a new geopolitical entity under a new political, ethnic, economic, and constitutional order (Dedijer, 1981). On November 29, 1943, a new state came into being on the political map of central Europe—the Socialist Federated Republic of Yugoslavia. The effect on the women's movement and women's issues was dramatic.

During the 45 years of socialist Yugoslavia, three rather distinct phases in women's social activism are evident (Soljan, 1979; Tomsic, 1981). In the early years of 1942 to 1953, Tito's Communist party activated women in its partisan war against the German and Italian fascist military forces; this was an important phase in women's revolutionary action. Women became self-organized in 1942 under a single umbrella organization, the Antifascist Front of Women, and about 100,000 women (mostly working class) joined or supported Tito's partisans. The ideological leaders of this women's movement were popular, charismatic personalities—mostly members or supporters of the Communist party such as Kata Pejnovic, a peasant woman from Croatia with great insight into women's issues (Soljan-Bakaric, 1977). The core ideology of this first-wave socialist women's movement was rooted, in many respects, in the tradition of the flourishing prewar local voluntary groups in the rural and urban areas.

From an organizational point of view (Kornhauser, 1959), the prime mission of the Antifascist Front of Women was to promote a multitude of local, small, independent, and socially responsive "cells" of women, each working toward meeting the larger societal needs of the community. In the late 1940s to early 1950s, the organization, including some 2,000 local branches, focused on such "specific problems" as developing alternative approaches to child care, providing health education and counseling to women and parents, and creating alternative community resources for workers' families. The organization of these local branches was multilevel, originating with the local communes, including the municipalities, and culminating at the federal–national level.

A shift in the mission of the Antifascist Front of Women between 1953 and 1961 represents the second phase of women's activism under socialism. The movement became identified with the political socialist establishment, and by 1961 the organization had changed its name to the Socialist Conference of Yugoslav Women (SCOW). During this phase, the leadership consisted mainly of the women associated with Yugoslavia's new class (Djilas, 1957)—primarily the wives of military officers and the wives of local political leaders. The organization became smaller, because women from a broader base were now no longer involved. It supported Tito's program. In the first phase of activism, volunteerism in women's community actions, such as helping the poor, was regarded as the rule. However, in the second phase women who remained active in community matters by and large were motivated by social power rather than philanthropic motives.

During the third phase, from the 1960s to 1990, as the Socialist Conference of Yugoslav Women became identified with the political–ideological establishment, women's social activism underwent a period of dormancy. The organization did not respond directly to women's issues in any substantial way; rather, it remained active only in political organizations and local branches of the state legislature, with a broad political agenda.

Furthermore, during Tito's era, there were salient changes in Yugoslav socialist society over which women's organizations, even official ones, had no substantial control. It is important to note that during this period these organizations never asked for control, even on the basis of their constitutional rights as defined in the Constitution of the Socialist Federated Republic of Yugoslavia of 1976.

Gains versus Losses under Yugoslav State Socialism

During the 45 years of Yugoslav socialism, women achieved a great many gains in terms of social welfare, education, specialized health care for mothers and children, constitutional rights for employment, and beneficiary status at retirement—to name a few. In many respects, the economic and social status of women in socialist Yugoslavia was improved and their issues more readily recognized and accommodated, especially compared with their contemporaries in the other socialist countries of central Europe. This advancement can be attributed to the "special case" of Yugoslavia's early experimentation with modes of self-management, both as an economic order and as a strategy for empowering local policy-making (Furtak, 1978; Kardelj, 1978; Tomsic, 1981).

In counterpoint, during the Yugoslav socialist era a great many women's issues were poorly handled. Even within the Yugoslav system of "self-management," women's labor in the Balkans remained largely marginalized and exploited. For example, large-scale political campaigns targeted women to become part of the working class but provided them with the lowest-paying jobs, which had been abandoned by men. In short, when compared to men, women were heavily discriminated against both in their career development and in their wages (Bejakovic, 1991; Gattin, 1990).

In summary, the women's movement in the era of Yugoslav socialism showed many dualities. On the positive side, a great many women stayed involved in everyday politics and were active in promoting women's rights both on a national and an international level. In contrast with the presocialist era, women's voluntary activism now was lodged within the broader framework of the socialist system. On the negative side, however, the movement during this time never aimed at becoming a broad-based populist women's movement but, rather, stayed within the confines of a political elite involved with causes other than women's issues. Thus, Yugoslavia's socialist women's movement, in contrast to its prewar origins, failed to become the driving force for large-scale voluntary action and did not promote women's basic rights for economic equality with men (Versa, 1991).

Current Context: The 1990s

With the death of Tito in 1980 came a period of instability in socialist Yugoslavia. However, the major death blow occurred with the political upheavals that took place in all of Eastern Europe's socialist countries in the 1990s. As Yugoslavia split into separate nation states, its political changes were accompanied by nationalistic–ethnic changes. The state of Croatia now is faced not only with political evolution, but also with the economic and social consequences of war.

Currently, there is a whirlpool of many ideological, political, and social subcultures in Croatia. Political polarization ranges from neoromantic longings for the "good old socialist times" to hard-driving beliefs invested in a free market economy. In the population at large, many Croatians fear that this new political development will take the form of a quasi-democracy in that one single party—the Croatian Democratic Community (HDZ)—will have most of the political power. Yet the people also are exhausted and drained by the national and international political manipulations and have little energy to deal with this issue.

At the same time, needless to say, the outbreak and escalation of war in the former Yugoslavia has placed enormous stress on the Republic of Croatia. Currently, Croatia is an economically devastated country. The following statistics illustrate the enormity of the problem:

About 40 percent of Croatia's prewar industrial capacity has been physically destroyed by heavy military bombing. About 350,000 homes have been destroyed. Only 1.2 million of a total of 4.7 million people are employed; 200,000 people are registered as unemployed. The average net salary for working women amounts to 300 dinars ($200), a drastic drop from an average 1990 monthly wage of 1,000 dinars (approximately $600).

Furthermore, according to recent statistics, Croatia's social welfare system is caring for 265,400 displaced people and for an additional population of 363,400 people from the territories of former Yugoslavia. Croatia's expenses for the refugee programs from its own territories alone amount to about 20 percent of total national income. In addition, Croatia has a population of over 750,000 retired civilians whose pensions, by now, average less than 40 dinars ($30) per month, far below subsistence level. The total material casualties of Croatia in this war have been estimated at $20 billion. In the words of a local economist, "Even if everything gets better, there is no doubt that the forthcoming months shall be extremely difficult for the citizenry of Croatia. This is the time for survival, and not for life" (Juresko, 1992, p. 3a).

Not surprisingly, a considerable increase in serious urban and rural social problems is predicted to occur within the next five years. These problems are expected to include juvenile delinquency, drug abuse, abuse and neglect of women and children, lack of care for elderly and chronically ill people, alcoholism, vagrancy, and prostitution (Petak, 1991). In addition, it is estimated that about two-thirds of the total population will be affected by posttraumatic stress disorder. For example, recent research showed that only one of 10 children from the war-torn areas of the country (for example, Slavonia) could be assessed as psychologically unimpaired from a clinical point of view (Barath, 1992b).

Case Study: The Women's Alliance of Croatia

WAC has been selected as the case study for this chapter, because it illustrates current developments in women's issues. WAC is not a newly founded organization; rather, it is an organization whose origins date back to 1939, the era of presocialist Croatia (Soljan, 1979). Thus, the organization represents the historical and cultural continuity of women's movements throughout the turbulent past of Croatian society.

Furthermore, this particular organization has kept the continuity of the liberal–social democratic tradition of many of the women's movements of the presocialist era. It should be noted that left-wing women's organizations are a rarity in today's environment as mass political behavior is moving back toward neoclericalism and neoconservatism.

This case study provides an opportunity from both a political and a sociological point of view, to examine what is happening to traditionally leftist women's movements of the socialist societies of central Europe in the midst of turbulent democratic transitions. Data for this study were obtained from WAC documents and from interviews with representatives of WAC leadership (personal communication with A. Racan, August 1992).

Organizational Beginnings—Organizational Mission

WAC emerged in spring 1990, at the time of a collision between the political desire for democratic changes in the western republics of former Yugoslavia (Slovenia and Croatia) and the rising Bolshevik/ethnofascist totalitarianism in its eastern areas (Serbia and Montenegro). This ideological split had reached the Zagreb headquarters of the Socialist Conference of Women of Yugoslavia, the last formal national women's organization inherited from socialist Yugoslavia. In opposition to the political "elite" of the organization, who retained a commitment to the communist ideology of former Yugoslavia, was a handful of women in subordinate roles who had strong democratic attitudes and strong cultural bonds to their local communities or territories. As it evolved, the leaders with strong pro-Yugoslavian, communist ideology left the Zagreb headquarters. Those who stayed became the founders of a new, independent women's organization—WAC—devoted to women's issues on a nonpartisan and innovative basis.

The vast majority of organizers were professional women—lawyers, economists, physicians, and social scientists—who had long-range goals to develop community action groups throughout the country, according to the earlier model of the voluntary action groups in the first decades of this century.

WAC's founding document was created in April 1990 by a group consisting of approximately 15 to 20 women and men:

> *Women's Alliance of Croatia is a nonpolitical social organization. That means, we invite all people who are willing to work for the causes of this Alliance, regardless of nationality, ideological, political, or religious self-determination. We offer membership to individuals, local community organizations, women's activities and clubs, professional associations, as well as interest communities and other organizations.* True equity for women is the cornerstone to all and any human society [emphasis added]. (Women's Alliance of Croatia, 1990, p. 1)

WAC is unique as a national umbrella organization aimed at developing a clearinghouse for women's nonprofit organizations in Croatia. The clearinghouse serves as both an information and a support center. WAC is not designed to be a grassroots, local, community-based action group.

The first major public program of the organization was a conference organized in response to the newly prepared constitution of the Republic of Croatia, after the first multiparty elections in May 1990. The core mission of this important convention, with approximately 600 participants from regional and local community centers, was to open a debate and critical analysis of the Republic's new constitution, including recommendations for perspectives on women's issues. One of the main goals was to provide recommendations for policy-making concerning marriage and the family.

Another critical issue was the ever-worsening economic situation for women—a clear gender-discriminatory process. Empirical evidence suggested that for the last two fiscal years (1988 and 1989), the ratio between the genders on the list of the unemployed, a pool of some 145,000 to 150,000 people, represented a 59 percent bias toward women (Petrovic, 1990).

Last, for the first time the issue of abortion became a clear dividing line between those people with liberal attitudes and those with clerical attitudes. The issue became impassioned not only because of its ethical significance regarding women's rights, but also because it represents a strong area of disagreement among political parties. The politicalization of this issue, in fact, has served to obscure its deep moral significance as a women's issue.

Parenthetically, it should be noted that while the basic attitude of WAC on abortion remains protective of women's basic rights of self-determination, another women's nonprofit organization—the "Croatian Women"— has been resurrected from its presocialist past. The Croatian Women have rather proclerical–ethnocentric objectives, taking a stand opposite WAC on many issues, including abortion , thus highlighting one of the leading ethical dilemmas of our times (that is, Hrvtska Zenao).

Organizational Goals

WAC's founding document calls attention to the achievements made in the former socialist era that should be maintained and also identifies issues that either were never raised or were never resolved (Women's Alliance of Croatia, 1990). The goals demonstrate primarily a commitment to social change, with mere implications for provision of services.

Goals in the social policy arena, developed either in presocialist or socialist Yugoslavia, that have been articulated by WAC and codified as women's constitutional rights, include

- equality of people under the law

- legal protection of women and family

- social welfare benefits for women and family

- women's rights in birth control (abortion)

- women's rights in family planning

- quality health care for mother and child

- equal opportunity in science and the arts

- support for the United Nations Children's Fund in children's rights.

A second set of goals also has been identified: those that have been articulated in the past but that have not reached final codification into law. These goals, which were espoused in the previous era of socialist Yugoslavia but require continued political work, include

- flexible work schedules and leave for women

- a raise in family income after the birth of each child

- health promotion for elderly and disabled people.

An additional internally focused organizational goal is that of improving WAC's relationship with the media.

WAC has articulated a new set of goals, evolving from current needs that are not only quite specific but also identify broader policy issues affecting women and family life:

- more women's rights in decision making (in family planning and in political, economic, social, and health matters)

- more political representatives serving women's interests

- equal employment opportunity

- special social services for working women

- comprehensive care for children

- paid work leave for child-related problems

- equal access to kindergarten as a basic need

- whole-day school program for all children

- promotion of women's rights in village rural settings

- programs against domestic violence

- peace and nonviolence in the neighborhood

- programs against ethnic and related conflicts

- respect toward women in the mass media

- protection of human well-being as a basic need.

These 14 new goals represent causes that were not advanced under the former socialist regime but that are important in the upcoming times for democratic change. And these goals are oriented toward systems change, even in a time of great crisis and personal need.

Critical Actors

In the past, women's voluntary action on these issues always emerged with a combination of two kinds of leadership. On the one hand, there has always been a core group of highly educated women with expertise in politics, public law, social policy, and public health who are active both in local universities and universities throughout Europe (Belica, Cecuk, & Skrbic, 1984). On the other hand, there have been activists at the local grassroots level. To date, while most activity has evolved through the efforts of the former group, it is expected that there will be an increase in the local community action of women through the many underground feminist and women's alternative organizations that surely will reemerge, reflecting both a historical and a moral tradition in these territories. This group consists of an enormous population of both professional and semi-professional women (for example, some 30,000 medical nurses), all of whom were, until now, repressed and depressed in their personal, professional, and public lives.

Resources

Currently, WAC is run totally on a voluntary basis; it has no paid employees. This situation is not unusual in Croatia because this has always been the reality, even in the presocialist era. The notion of volunteerism in traditional societies such as Croatia has been rooted in community action projects rather than in self-centered personal interests. Therefore, the resources were always drawn from the community (for example, church, court, political party) and not from private donations or the door-to-door fundraising common in American society. This practice reflects a basic value (communal responsibility) in this society. Thus, there are some 2,000 activists throughout the country who do whatever they can in their "spare time."

Specifically, there are two things implied here. First, WAC has no stable financial support. Second, given the heritage of the Yugoslav socialist infrastructure, there are only two paths for raising funds that are still possible. One is asking for government support in subsidizing visible and important action projects, such as editing a professional journal, organizing women's conferences, or setting up exhibitions for art exhibits at local schools. The other path is asking the for-profit sector (for example, the pharmaceutical industry, tobacco companies, soft drink manufacturers) to sponsor specific projects. The quid pro quo is the expectation that nonprofit organizations will promote the business and its products. Neither path has been taken by WAC, and it has not yet addressed the financial problems directly. There is some thought to using the professional journal it publishes, *Zena*, as an income source.

Autonomy

Liberal thinking tends to be suppressed, almost devastated, at the current time in Croatia. Therefore, the issue of organizational autonomy in the social and political context of Croatia is a sheer philosophical abstraction. The social reality is that women live hard and work hard in an environment that is harsher than ever before. They work about 16 to 18 hours a day to cope with inflation and overall misery in personal, family, and professional life. The total financial expenses for school materials for a first-grade child, for instance, are twice as much as the monthly salary of a blue-collar worker. In an economic situation where the average family income is about 100 dinars (approximately $70), it is a political abstraction, if not a social illusion, to talk about "autonomy," "freedom," "democracy," or any political goals set by Western societies that have no historical experience or understanding about life in central Europe for the past few decades.

Autonomy and self-reliance are a lifestyle still to be learned in this society, and autonomy may have political connotations here that differ from those in the United States. Many people fear that the much praised transition to a free market economy may lead, among other things, to the government's abandoning of its own responsibility for a great many social welfare problems. These are fundamental public issues that are unrelated to nonprofit or self-help activity.

Controversies

There are two controversial women's issues in present-day Croatia, both of which are of central importance to WAC. First, there is a controversy regarding family planning—specifically, women's rights for personal integrity and self-determination, including the abortion issue mentioned earlier. The debate about abortion serves to represent the broader political causes that are dividing the entire population, rather than promote open democratic dialogue among social groups with different moral attitudes and social responsibilities related to the issue itself. There is an ever-growing lack of communication between two orthodoxies. There is the historical stereotype that confines women to the traditional roles of "mother and housewife," and there is the equally rigid stereotype of the "liberated woman" who has assumed sole responsibility for her own well-being and nothing beyond. The social reality certainly should lie somewhere between these two extremes.

Second, there is a controversy regarding the economic valuation of women's labor, either within or outside the household. This issue is of vital significance because there is, on the upcoming social and economic policy agenda, a debate regarding the surplus of workers with administrative and technological expertise in the present labor force. The victims of any new social policy are likely to be the thousands of women who make up over 80 percent of all those employed in government agencies, in the services industry, and in professions that are experiencing high rates of unemployment (such as law, medicine, and education).

The key factor to this "double-bind" social reality, apparently, is in the organization and economic valuation of women's labor, both in terms of the work done at home and the work performed in the workplace. At the present time, the paradox is that women labor for 16 to 18 hours a day, both at home and in the workplace, yet their work is unpaid at home and underpaid at work. This is one of the major issues in which WAC is likely to invest most of its intellectual and moral resources in the years to come.

Services

Given the current political realities, the primary areas of activity in WAC at this time are the provision of emergency services. However, in addition to the provision of direct services, WAC's Zagreb headquarters has become the crisis center for the enormous number of emergency situations related to the war. These situations include a range of activities, such as organizing and distributing humanitarian aid at the time when international aid was virtually unavailable, as well as providing a basis for the first peace movement, known as the "Wall of Love," composed of several hundred thousand mothers whose sons were captured by the Yugoslav Federal Army.

One of the most interesting action programs sponsored by WAC was organized in early September 1991. It involved inception and installation of a psychological-counseling telephone hot line for refugees, displaced families, and all other citizens in need of help in these territories. The hot line is staffed by dozens of women volunteers from the mental health professions, including social workers, psychologists, and family therapists. According to an empirical survey (Lugomer-Armano, 1991), at its inception about 75 percent of all service users were women. Male users mainly asked for information, whereas women asked both for information and for advice at about equal rates. The hot line is still operating.

There is also activity at the local level; action projects, such as "Dubrovkinje," a women's community action project in Dubrovnik, "Puljanke" in Pula, and "Splicanke" in Split, have started mushrooming all over Croatia. The national leadership of WAC maintains, in accordance with the organization's mission, that there is no need to centralize the initiatives of these local community action groups, because the local leadership best understands the priority human needs at the local level. What the local projects need most, however, is support in the form of information, advice, moral backing, professional help, and transfer of organizational knowledge and skills. "What women did throughout these rather invisible community action projects in the past two years was to help their own communities survive the horrors of this war, both physically and psychologically" (personal communication with A. Racan, August 1992).

In summary, the outbreak of war against Croatia meant a crisis situation for WAC. This newly reborn organization became visible and—for the first time—indispensable in responding to rapidly growing human needs of millions of people facing misery, mass killing, and genocide (Judas & Kostovic, 1992; Lay, 1992; U.S. Committee for Refugees, 1992). WAC is also planning for the future, the postwar period of this society, with a plan that focuses on poverty. The program, called "SAVENA," is a comprehensive action program for social welfare counseling and home visits to poor families in the Zagreb area, initially. The major aims of the program are to cope with economic, social, psychological, and health problems in present wartime circumstances and in the upcoming postwar years.

SAVENA and other such programs

- raise funds for creating playrooms for preschool children, including special rooms run in different languages (for example, Slovenian, English, Italian, German) in addition to rooms for music, visual arts, and drama

- organize training courses for professional rehabilitation or prequalification of the unemployed, including courses for professional advancement in business administration, marketing, physiotherapy, and small household services; courses for resuming "old-time handwork" such as repairing old watches, furniture, jewelry, and the like; training for public services such as waitressing in restaurants; and much more

- create telemedia consulting networks for women that focus on their legal, social, psychological, family, and mental health problems.

In the realm of activities that focus on public law and public policy, special services will be provided in the near future that include legal courses on employment and work, inheritance and ownership, tax reporting, and traffic violations and counseling on retirement and pensions and family law.

Advocacy

In discussing advocacy, the leaders of WAC gave a short but strong moral answer: "In the midst of this wartime, we found ourselves in a preempted space, in a vacuum of innovative ideas for advocacy. After all, there are many, too many, controversial designs for social development in the country, so you are numbed as to where to start!" (staff interview, July, 1992). The reality is an urgent requirement to provide social services to meet immediate needs; attention to advocacy must be put on the back burner. Despite the many qualifications and rationales offered, there appears to be a rather well-formed action program with which WAC's intellectual leadership plans to enter the postwar transition period of this society.

Chances for Survival?

The core message of WAC's leadership can be summarized in a single phrase: "self-reliance and self-help." Unlike women's organizations in Western nations, women's social movements in these territories have no experience in developing appropriate infrastructures for their organizations and lack managerial skills and experience in lobbying. In addition, there is no substantial tradition of organizing and supporting self-help–mutual aid groups, such as those that exist and flourish in the Western world (Barath, 1992a).

Added to the complexity is the problem that this society is not rich enough to depend on private donations from its own citizens for the support of nonprofit organizations. This reality must also be linked to the history of this republic. The entire economic structure of this society still retains much of its socialist past, with an emphasis on a government-run economy.

At the moment, it appears that there are only a few approaches to facilitate the organizational survival of WAC. One method is to gain economic independence through the use of its own public media, such as the professional journal *Zena*. Another approach is to get truly involved in the newly emerging operation of innovative human services, as planned for by SAVENA.

The rather strong moral tradition of the organization sets up specific criteria. These include the expectation of well-designed projects, use of high-quality personnel, and, above all, maintenance of the highest possible moral standards of "market behavior" for these services. The goal is to meet the best interests of the 2.5 million women of this country.

Conclusion

There are three major lessons offered in this case study of WAC. First, women's issues and movements in these territories, that is, Croatia, have a special historical background rooted in a concept of equity relations between the genders. These cultural codes were in operation for decades preceding the emergence of state socialism after World War II. These patterns were then co-opted and systematically "burned out," along with many other cultural traditions.

Second, the recent collapse of socialist Yugoslavia meant a challenge to one of Croatia's oldest social democratic women's organizations—WAC (Savez zena Hrvatske)—to become independent of everyday politics and to transform itself into a voluntary association with more responsibility in meeting basic human needs.

Last, one may expect the emergence of a rather complex and intensive interaction between the newly developing political democracy and emerging contemporary nonprofit organizations, such as WAC. However, as the example of WAC would suggest, the absence of an economically strong and legally well-defined nonprofit sector in the present Republic of Croatia and the absence of any legal provisions in its constitution make the entire voluntary sector fragile, organizationally ambiguous, and—from a policy-making perspective—marginal.

The challenge for present and future generations of Croatian women, as well as for the broad citizenry, is to learn more about political and social democracy to strengthen the possibility of a democratic society. Additionally, the citizenry will be challenged to learn more about models for organizational development, not only to assure the survival of organizations such as WAC but also to strengthen the nonprofit sector as a whole (Cnaan, Kang, & Perlmutter, 1992; Salamon, 1987; Van Til, 1981).

References

Barath, A. (1992a). *Patterns of helping and social support in American self-help groups: Cross-cultural perspectives.* Baltimore: Johns Hopkins University, Institute for Policy Studies.

Barath, A. (1992b). *Self-help groups of mothers with small children among the refugees from Croatia and Bosnia-Herzegovina: A project proposal to the UNICEF.* Unpublished manuscript.

Bejakovic, P. (1991). Razlozi povecane aktivnosti zena u razvijenim zemljama. *Zena, 49*(4–6), 2231.

Belica, B., Cecuk, L., & Skrbic, M. (Eds.). (1984). *Medicinski facultet sveucilista u Zagrebu.* Zagreb: Stvarnost.

Cnaan, R. A., Kang, C. H., & Perlmutter, F. D. (1992, March). *Voluntary associations: Societal variations in response to human needs.* Paper presented at ARNOVA conference, Indianapolis.

Dedijer, V. (1981). *Novi prolizi za biografiju Josipa Broza Tita.* (Vols. 1–2). Rijeka: GRA "Liburnija."

Djilas, M. (1957). *The new class.* New York: Praeger.

Erlich, V. (1978). *U drustvu s covjekom: Tragom njegovih kulturnih i socijalnih tekovina.* Zagreb: Sveucilisna naklada Liber.

Furtak, R. K. (1978). Yugoslavia: A special case. In J. E. Haward & R. N. Berki (Eds.), *State & society in contemporary Europe* (pp. 158–178). Oxford: Martin Robertson.

Gattin, K. (1990). Diskriminacija zena pri zaposljavanju. *Zena, 48* (3–4), 59–72.

Ivsic, M. (1936). *Diljem sela.* Zagreb: Hrvatsko knjizevno drustvo Sv. Jeronima.

Judas, M., & Kostovic, I. (Eds.). (1992). *Mass killing and genocide in Croatia 1991/92: A book of evidence.* Zagreb: Hrvatska Sveucilisna Naklada.

Juresko, G. (1992, August 30). Prezivljavanje, a ne zivot. *Novi Vjesnik - Zagreb,* 3A.

Kardelj, E. (1978). *Praci razvoja politickog sistema socijalistickog samopuravljanja.* Beograd: Komunist.

Kecman, J. (1978). *Zene Jugoslavije u radnickom pokretu i zenskim organizacijama 1918–1941.* Beograd: Narodna knjiga: Institut za savremenu istoriju.

Kornhauser, E. (1959). *The politics of mass society.* Glencoe, IL: Free Press.

Kotruljevic, B. (1458/1573). *Della mercantura es del mercante Perfetto. Libro Quatro. Utilismi ad agni mergante, Con privilegio.* In Venecia: All Élefanta. (Croatian translation: Z. Muljacic: O trgovini i o svarsenom trgaovcu. Cettiri knjige Gospaga Bene Gtoruljevica Dubrovcanina. U. Dubrovniku, 1989. JAZA.)

Lay, V. (Ed.). (1992). *Obzori opstanka: Ratna razaranja okoline u Hrvatskoj 1991.* Zagreb: Zelena akcija Zagreb.

Lugomer-Armano, G. (1991). Telefon za psiholosku pomoc u ratnim uvjetima. *Zena, 49*(4–6).

Petak, O. (1991). Zlostavljanje i zanemarivanje djece kao socijalni problem. *Zena, 49*(4–6), 32–40.

Petrovic, J. A. (1990). Zaposlenost-nezaposlenost zena u 1990. godini. *Zena, 48*(5–6), 59–65.

Salamon, L. M. (1987). Partners in public service: The scope and theory of government-nonprofit relations. In W. Powell (Ed.), *The nonprofit sector: Research handbook* (pp. 99–117). New Haven, CT: Yale University Press.

Soljan, M. (Ed.). (1979). *Zenski svijet.* Zagreb: Konferencija zena RK SSRNH.

Soljan-Bakaric, M. (Ed.). (1977). *Kata Pejnovic: Monografija.* Zagreb: Ognjen Prica.

Tomsic, V. (1981). *Zena u razvoju sociajalisticke samoupravne Jugoslavije.* Beograd: Jugoslavenska stvarnost.

U.S. Committee for Refugees. (1992, February). *Yugoslavia torn asunder: Lessons for protecting refugees from civil war.* Washington, DC: 1992 American Council for Nationalities Service.

Van Til, J. (1981). Volunteering and democratic theory. In J. D. Harman (Ed.), *Volunteerism in the eighties* (pp. 199–220). Washington, DC: University Press of America.

Versa, D. (1991). Lik zene u crtanom humoru. *Zena, 49*(1), 21–26.

Women's Alliance of Croatia. (1990). *Founding Declaration.* Zagreb: WAC.

Author's Notes

This study is part of a larger research project on voluntarism, started in 1990, that was designed to focus on the rather turbulent history of women's nonprofit organizations in the former socialist countries of central Europe. Unfortunately, this broader project is inactive now because of lasting war in our homeland. Therefore, the material presented should be taken as a global framework and challenge for more in-depth empirical study in other countries, under different conditions, and above all, in peace.

CHAPTER FIVE

Denmark

From Fringe to Paragovernmental Status

Kurt Klaudi Klausen

The Welfare State and the Third Sector

Nordic Countries and the Scandinavian Welfare State

The development of the Danish welfare state has been made possible by
a steady and accumulative economic growth throughout this century,
notably from the 1950s. A widespread consensus exists both to the present
social system of the welfare state and to the changes that are currently
taking place involving private and voluntary nonprofit organizations in
the provision of social services.

To understand the evolution of social and political consensus, it is
beneficial to look at three distinct historical features (discussed at length
in Klausen, 1992): (1) Denmark is a country of relative racial, social, and
economic homogeneity; (2) there is a tradition for peaceful and nonviolent policy development and conflict resolution supported by the workers' movement; and (3) there has been a pragmatic professionalization of
administrative and political decision making since World War II (Klausen,
1982, 1986, 1989; K. Nielsen & Pedersen, 1989b).

Together these features ensure that no substantial disagreements and
disputes occur over central values and goals regarding the present welfare system. This is facilitated by the fact that Danish society is based on
solidaristic values, mutuality, and trust, which can be traced back to the
end of the 19th century, to the peasant movement and their cooperative
arrangements, and to the social democratic ideology of the workers' movement and the social democratic party.

Denmark is a rich country, but what matters when analyzing welfare
states is not wealth but the way different welfare components are produced and how wealth and welfare are redistributed among the citizens.
There are a number of ways to distinguish between different models of

welfare states stressing different dimensions. One such model can be developed as a combination of the models of Wilensky and Libeaux (1958) and Titmuss (1974). This "institutional model" describes the Scandinavian countries as nations who consider it to be the responsibility of the state through state institutions to take care of social problems—not the responsibility of individuals or private institutions (Flora, 1986; Johansen & Kolberg, 1985; Kuhnle & Selle, 1990).

On a continuum from states dependent on voluntary agencies, such as The Netherlands, to countries with a mixed distribution of public and voluntary provision, such as the United States, to countries dependent on public agencies, the Scandinavian countries (and notably Sweden) belong to the latter (Kramer, 1981). The role of the Scandinavian welfare state has been not only to secure the rights of citizens and a number of collective goods such as infrastructure and military but also to redistribute wealth among the citizens by a graduated system of taxation and to provide education, social security, and health treatment by public agencies. The Danish and Scandinavian welfare states are characterized by the following traits (Ericson et al., 1987; Kuhnle, 1989; Kuhnle & Solheim, 1985; K. Nielsen & Pedersen, 1989a; Togeby & Svensson, 1991):

- a relatively large public sector that is looked on as legitimate, with many people working in public welfare provision

- a relatively high decentralization of the actual spending on and production of services in health, education, and social security

- a high degree of provisions based on universality and rights

- a relatively successful redistribution of wealth from the richest to the poorest

- a less polarized class-society in which the overall attitude and important political negotiations are based on consensus rather than conflict

The Expansion of the Public Sector

The public sector is large in the Scandinavian countries and has been growing since the 1960s. In Denmark public expenditures rose from 25 percent to 60 percent of the gross national product (GNP) from 1960 to 1985. Social expenditures rose drastically through the 1970s in all the Nordic countries: from an average of 15 percent of GNP in 1970 to about 30 percent of GNP in Denmark and Sweden and 24 percent in Norway and Finland, and from 10 percent to 15 percent in Iceland. However, this expansion of the public spending stagnated during the 1980s (Nordic Statistical Secretariat, 1986/1987).

Three important factors may account for the expansion of the public sector. These factors reveal the dynamics of a new social differentiation, and they must be seen within the context of a number of profound socio-economic changes that took place from the 1950s to the 1970s and involved the decrease of the rural population and the expansion of the towns in the 1950s and 1960s, the economic boom of the 1960s, and the economic recession of the 1970s and 1980s. First, women have become a more active part of the work force (partly because they were needed as a supplementary work force during the expansion of the late 1960s and the beginning of the 1970s). Second, the percentage of elderly people has risen. Third, the private economy has experienced a recession or, more correctly, has not been able to increase activities at the same rate at which the work force has increased; therefore, the rate of unemployment rose throughout the 1970s and 1980s (although the number of people employed during the 1980s was at an all-time high). The high numbers of people currently employed make it necessary for someone other than family members to care for children and the elderly; furthermore, unemployment seems to deepen the social problems of families and individuals, and the total result is increased public spending. In addition, the institutional political climate has to favor public welfare provision; the growth in public spending is not just an automatic reflection of changed needs (Budgetdepartementet Udgiftsanalyser, 1990).

From Mixed to Negotiated Economy

Recent political analyses of Danish and Scandinavian society suggest that there has been a change from the mixed economy of the 1950s toward a negotiated economy during the 1980s and 1990s (Hernes, 1985; K. Nielsen & Pedersen, 1989b). The emergence of the negotiated economy is characterized by a dissolution of the autonomous spheres of the state and the market and by prices and wages being determined as a result of negotiations in public institutions involving a number of autonomous groups and individuals. The transformation from a mixed to a negotiated economy can be found in all the Scandinavian countries (K. Nielsen & Pedersen, 1989a).

The emerging politico–administrative system is characterized by the widespread consensus among the contending interest groups that are co-opted into forming professional networks in and among segments of the state system. The consensus regarding both the welfare state as a system and the market economy as the prime force in the development of society is established through negotiations in which the professional representatives are developing a common institutional setting, comprising a common language and a set of shared norms and values (Pedersen, 1988).

The explanatory strength and novelty of the concept of the negotiated economy has to do with its institutional approach. Through institutional changes, new initiatives like the centers for women become an accepted alternative and supplement to public services, and through the negotiated economic system, these initiatives influence public policy and receive public funding.

When analyzing the development of society, the political decision making, and the production and distribution of welfare services, it is possible to overlook some crucial mechanisms in Danish society that are located neither within the realm of the public nor the private for-profit sector. This is not an exclusive omission by Danish economists and political scientists. Even an attempt to describe a welfare mix fails to or refrains from distinguishing voluntary and nongovernmental organizations as something different from the state, the market, and the household (Rose, 1986).

The Third (and Fourth) Sectors

As defined by Hood and Schuppert (1988), paragovernmental organizations are "all types of organizations other than core public bureaucracies which are used to provide public services" (p. 1). Historically, Denmark has distinguished among the large philanthropic and charity organizations (including religious organizations like the Church Army, the Salvation Army, and the Blue Cross); the large secular organizations, many of which were formed between the wars, that work to the benefit of particular groups (including associations for elderly and disabled people); and newer, less-institutionalized grassroots organizations and self-help groups that deal with specific problems and have idealistic goals, such as the centers for battered and abused women. All of these organizations depend on private and public funding and on volunteer staffs. But many of these (initially often more independent and voluntary based) associations have been transformed into highly institutionalized, publicly financed, self-governing institutions managing public affairs. This, however, is not new; cooperation with the state has strong historical roots. Furthermore, this development may be interpreted as the result of a deliberate strategy of the voluntary and nonprofit associations.

Paragovernmental Organizations and the Growth of the Welfare State

Until the mid-18th century, mutual associations were the only alternative to poor (state) relief for those who became ill or were disabled, unemployed, or elderly. The state had not yet created institutions to compensate for the loss of the close relationships characterizing local communities and guilds. This situation gradually changed during the second half of the 18th century as the social laws made it possible for the state to support the private and voluntary associations (H. Hansen, 1930; Nørregaard, 1930, 1943; Warmdahl, 1930). For example, there were 26,000 members of some 300 sick benefit associations in 1866, and 120,000 members in about 1,000 associations in 1885, but it was not until 1887 that the state recognized this work by supporting the health insurance society with funding of 50 percent on a help to self-help basis (Nørregaard, 1930).

The growth rate in new associations follows changes in society. Buksti and Johansen (1979) concluded their survey by pointing out the relationship between

- industrialization and the creation of a number of workers' and employees' associations (in the 1890s and the beginning of the 20th century)

- new agricultural associations and the political regulation in the 1930s, the 1960s, and the 1970s (as a result of Danish membership in the European Community)

- new associations in the field of industry and trade and the political regulation during World War I and in the 1930s and 1940s

- the creation of social and humanitarian associations and the creation of the welfare state.

The rapid growth in social and humanitarian associations is intimately connected with the creation of the modern welfare state. Clearly, private welfare provision in Denmark (Klausen, 1991) is a part of, functions as an alternative or complement to, and supplements the welfare state and should rightly not be conceived of as a negation of this system.

As mentioned earlier, many of the voluntary and nonprofit organizations, from the 1930s on, had as a deliberate policy not only to gain public support but also to make the state take over as many of their obligations as possible (Habermann, 1987). This strategy succeeded with the creation of the modern welfare state, but it did not make these private institutions superfluous. On the contrary, private institutions took up new obligations and expanded their activity in cooperation with the welfare state. Much of the development of the welfare state is a result of public support to private self-governing institutions as an outgrowth of changes in the social laws in 1933 that made it possible for the state and the local governments to make contracts with private institutions for welfare provision. Thus, public authorities were granted representation in the boards of the institutions provided they fulfilled certain minimum standards regarding accounting, number of clients, payment by clients, and general goals. In this way, the state expanded its influence to paragovernmental welfare provision.

The development in the 1970s must be seen in the context of the social reforms that were designed in the 1960s by the social commission. Together with the decentralization of welfare services to the local level, these laws were intended to bring the social authorities closer to their clients and to secure not only physical but also symbolic security. This grand idea was conceived under the impact of economic growth and was implemented and had functioned during a recession. In some instances, and for some groups of clients (battered and abused women, among others), the decentralization of welfare services was not without problems.

In his survey on indirect public administration in Denmark, Christensen (1988) concluded that there has been a wider use of indirect administrative subjects (defined as "[technically] a legal person apart from the state and the local governments, however, performing public activities," (p. 66) since World War II, so that they now account for an essential part of the public sector. He estimated the number of self-governing institutions and associations in 1985 at 3,992 and 85, respectively, out of 4,810 indirect administrative subjects; he estimated their total economic consumption at 82,081 million kroner (which was about 13 percent of the 1985 GNP of 613,000 million kroner). Of the 4,810 subjects, 2,766 were located in the social and health sector, consuming some 51,555 million kroner. Christensen concluded that the use of these social services organizations has grown in the social and health sector (together with the supply and transport service sector) since 1960 and that this trend will continue.

In this survey the social and health sector is broad, including the public assignments on the labor market and various pension schemes. This broad definition illustrates the difficulty of separating the private paragovernmental welfare provision by independent agencies from the pure state provision, because cash income transfers constitute the bulk of expenses of the welfare state in the social sector (Budgetdepartementet, 1990).

However, Christensen's (1988) findings are contradicted by another survey (Parsby, 1988) that examined the number of private and public institutions between 1980 and 1986, including kindergartens and institutions serving children, teenagers, adults from 18 to 67 years, and elderly people. Parsby's findings indicate a trend to close the private institutions and open new public institutions. This survey, however, does not examine whether new forms of private and public institutions are emerging.

The Scandinavian or institutional model allows nongovernmental and voluntary organizations to play only a minor role in the welfare provision if private nonprofit institutions heavily economically dependent on or on contract with the state in the public welfare provision are excluded. Otherwise, private or indirect public administration does play a considerable role (note that these organizations are being looked on by the Danes as public, not private, institutions). The growth of the welfare state, on the other hand, may be seen very much as the result of a deliberate policy by the voluntary and nonprofit institutions formed on the basis of a long tradition of intimate cooperation between them and the state.

Voluntary and nonprofit institutions on the fringe of this system function as alternatives to public organizations and supplements when needs are overlooked or deliberately excluded because the public social system is not able to handle them. Users of services provided by voluntary and nonprofit organizations are most often clients who are poor, unemployed, and uneducated but also include families who require shelter, day care, and nursing homes. Two of the major areas in which voluntary and nonprofit organizations have recently changed old or developed new institutions to meet unfulfilled needs are addiction and domestic violence. The remainder of this chapter discusses domestic violence.

Advisory Centers, Crises Centers, and Self-Help Groups

Role and Status of Women in Denmark

Since the late 19th century, Danish women have organized themselves to claim equal rights such as the right to vote (which was granted them as late as 1908 for local government elections and 1915 for elections to the parliament) and the claim for a just salary—a battle that is still being fought (Madsen, 1986). Whereas in the early years the women's movement (both the left and the right wings) seemed moderate in their actions, the movements of the 1970s and 1980s were more revolutionary, linking the fight for equal rights with the class struggle in general and the liberation of women in particular (Klausen & Mikkelsen, 1988).

In 1992, women constituted 51 percent of the population (all figures are from Statistisk Oversigt, 1992). Since 1940 the number of women working outside the home has grown. In 1992, 52 percent of Danish females were working outside the home, 22 percent were pensioners, 20 percent were children and students, and 6 percent were housewives, compared with 35 percent, 9 percent, 23 percent, and 33 percent, respectively, in 1940. Women still tend to have the most routine and least well-paid jobs, and they also work part-time more frequently than men (35 percent versus 10 percent). This probably explains why women do more domestic chores than men. The figures have changed though: Today men are more active at home. In 1976, 53 percent of the women did three-quarters of the housework; in 1987, 29 percent did. In 1976, 27 percent of the men did from 26 percent to 50 percent of the domestic chores; in 1987, 51 percent did. Furthermore, the equal participation is most pronounced in younger families and in families where women have full-time jobs. In families with small children (between birth and 6 years of age), 50 percent of the women work outside the home today; in 1980, 33 percent of them were working. In the 1990s couples tend to marry later, with the average well above 30 years for the first marriage. The percentage of marriages ending in divorce has grown dramatically throughout the 1960s, 1970s, and 1980s. A marked narrowing has occurred of the difference in education levels between men and women from 1980 to 1990. The percentage of female students enrolled in selected courses of education rose between 1980 and 1990 as follows:

- from 58 to 60 percent in general education at the upper level (similar to high school; 16 to 18 years of age)

- from 41 to 45 percent in vocational education at the second level (education that provides and improves working skills of 16- to 18-year-olds)

- from 48 to 51 percent in further education (universities and the like; age 19 to 25 years and older).

However, when looking at the distribution of men and women in further education, women are overrepresented in both the short-length (for example, preschool teacher; two or three years) and medium-length (for example, nurses and primary school teachers; three to four years) courses and in arts and music and health. The percentage of women elected to the parliament has been growing steadily from 8 percent in 1950 to 27 percent in 1984 and to 34 percent in 1990. A sign of the changed position of women may be that the coalition government that was formed and led by the Social Democrats in 1992 had eight female ministers out of 24.

Origin of Advisory Centers, Crises Centers, and Self-Help Groups

The social laws of the 1970s were designed in the hope that the state would be able to handle all social problems, but it soon became clear that this public system could not deal efficiently with all the needs of the citizens. In the slipstream of what is normally described as the crises of the welfare state (unemployment, social disintegration, and so forth), but what is in fact a socioeconomic crisis of society in general, problems inherent to modern society became more pronounced.

These problems, such as the breakup of families, the increased loneliness and lack of self-confidence among women, and the domestic problems between men and women and with children caused by unemployment and in connection with alcohol or drug abuse, became a heavy burden on the public social system. In many ways, the public system was not equipped to deal with these delicate personal matters. Moreover, apart from hospitals and police stations, public institutions are not fully operating and open to the public at night and on weekends (exactly the time when battered and abused women need assistance). Furthermore, people feel reluctant approaching public authorities both because public authorities are required to keep files about their clients and because of a general feeling of alienation and impersonalization when dealing with public bureaucracies.

During the 1980s the public sector did not expand its activities. Rather, modernization programs were designed to slim public expenditure, a trend that still results in cutbacks. As an example, the overall number of working hours in the social and health sector has decreased 5.6 percent from 1990 to 1991 (Danmarks Statistik, 1991). During this period, the voluntary and nonprofit organizations, such as the Salvation Army and the Blue Cross, continued and intensified their work, and new movements and groups came into existence to solve special problems and needs that the public social system did not seem able to handle.

Among these new groups were the "advisory centers for women," the "crises centers for women," and the "self-help centers." These centers were established during the 1980s to deal with problems of women. Men are not allowed entry to the crises centers. In the beginning that was also the case in the advisory centers, but this is no longer the situation there. Although the bulk of their clients are women, men and families often attend the advisory centers. The self-help groups are open to both men and women, but 80 percent of the participants are women. To analyze these organizations, Klausen and Evertsen (1992) made a general survey, conducted case studies and interviews, and gathered official reports and material from 15 centers throughout Denmark.

The way in which these centers came into existence is much the same. A specific need for support and service delivery (outside the public system) was recognized by a group of people (mostly women) who managed to organize themselves spontaneously, develop ad hoc practical solutions to their problems, and gain support to continue their endeavors. As an example, the creation of self-help centers that have been popping up since the late 1980s was spontaneous and coincidental. In Århus they came into existence because someone suggested to three women in an alternative "social boutique" that they begin a self-help group. The women (two "social advisers" and a "home nurse") thought it a good idea and put a small note in the local newspaper. More than 100 people showed up at the small boutique, so it was necessary to rethink and organize the whole thing before it was possible for the group to begin. A working group of 12 people was formed and during the next couple of months developed a framework for the organization that could coordinate and organize the initiatives.

Both the advisory and crises centers must be seen within the context of the grassroots movement and the women's movement in particular. Even if grassroots groups are characterized by their ability to unite people from different social groups and of different political observations, the value orientation of the women's movement of the 1970s and 1980s is to be found within the framework of the social democratic welfare state, with explicit solidaristic values (though with a more militant, revolutionary, and dogmatic touch in the 1970s than in the pragmatic latter half of the 1980s).

The new women's movement not only focused attention on equal political rights (as did the previous women's movement) but also took action to fight for the liberation of women from all oppression. This fight was against discrimination both at work and in the family and against the feminist image of women. To many this meant that the fight for women's rights was closely connected with socialistic ideals and class struggle. Furthermore, in some fractions of this movement, men became the incarnation of what women were fighting against (Flensted-Jensen, Frastein, & Pedersen, 1977; Giese, 1973; Klausen & Mikkelsen, 1988). The combination of the radical ideology with social action is what really put these organizations, at least in the beginning, on the fringe of society.

The women's movement created a public debate in which it became obvious that a need existed for centers for battered and abused women, because nowhere in the public system could these women anonymously seek shelter from brutal husbands or boyfriends at all hours. In this way, matters that were previously considered private or family issues, problems on the fringe of the public social system and of the public debate, became recognized as public concerns, accounting for the overall sympathy and public support they have received since.

The crises centers were established through the initiative of a group of women who in 1978 managed to occupy an old patrician house (the Countess Danner House) in the center of Copenhagen. The occupation lasted only a couple of days and was staged as a defense of the Countess Danner Foundation (formerly the King Frederik VII Foundation for women from the working class). The house was scheduled to be torn down. The occupation received considerable publicity and support from throughout the country. The politicians who wanted the house torn down gave in, and the women kept it. Throughout the country, women organized similar initiatives and collected money to support local endeavors. Initially, this was done on a voluntary basis and without public support, but it soon became necessary to employ someone in charge of coordinative and administrative duties. The advisory centers similarly spread quickly throughout the country. The advisory centers were started in 1983 on the initiative of a group of volunteers, among whom Hanne Reintoft (a former member of parliament for the Danish Communist party and widely recognized for work with social problems) was the leading figure. This group wanted to revitalize the idea of the public advisory centers that had been closed down with the introduction of the new social law in 1976 because they found that the new system could not handle the special problems of the women in question. However, they wanted the advisory centers to be private (self-governing) institutions.

Different Goals and Target Groups

The official goal of the advisory centers (their Danish name is *Mødrehjælpen* or "Help to mothers") is to help women with children and families with children under 18. In reality, these centers try to serve everyone who needs their help. Their primary function is to help and advise women who do not know how to handle problems and crises regarding housing, divorce, pregnancy prevention, pregnancy, grief, violence or abuse, incest, or separation. The centers serve people with all types of social problems relating to the family, including offering psychological assistance and economic and legal advice.

The goals of the crises centers are to give shelter to women and children, to cooperate with public authorities in solving and preventing such problems, and to make sure that society is informed about these problems. The target group of these centers is women in acute crises. However, the centers mainly help women who are dealing with either physical or psychological violence and terror. Some of the centers (for example, the one in Odense) restrict themselves to battered and abused women, because they do not have the means and resources to help women who need prolonged and complicated psychological assistance and because help for these women and women addicted to alcohol and other drugs is difficult to reconcile with the idea of self-help. These centers provide a place where women can seek shelter at all hours of the day, and stay, at times together with their children, for a night or even a considerable number of nights. In addition, they try to help and advise their clients on specific problems and arrange various cultural and enlightening activities.

The self-help centers are do-it-yourself groups in that they deal with all kinds of problems. The goals of the self-help centers are to help create networks where people can bring forward, discuss, and provide support for various personal problems. Groups are made up of people with similar problems; only people with severe problems (those who need the care of a psychologist or psychiatrist, those who might disrupt the group, or those who cannot participate actively in the group) are not allowed to participate. Every group is provided with a volunteer who tries to help the process get started and who eventually steps out when the group seems to be sufficiently self-supportive. Each group deals with specific topics, such as grief, anxiety, divorce, identity and self-consciousness, suicide, loneliness, and anorexia. Some of the groups are even more specific: groups helping widows whose husbands committed suicide, marriage with non-Danes, or women who love too much (for example, women who are married to substance abusers and who take on the responsibility and never think of themselves).

The guiding values of each of these groups are basically solidaristic, and in that sense they do not differ from the values of the larger society. However, the way in which they value the time and the personal concern for each client gives them an advantage over most public institutions. For example, examine the difference between the services a client would get in the advisory centers and in the public system. The public system and the social advisers there may be able to give a client some money, but they do not have the time to give personal advice. Rather, clients are often referred to the advisory centers, where each client receives an initial one-hour consultation with both a psychologist and a social adviser present, if necessary. The advisory centers provide this initial consultation to ensure that the total picture of the client's problems (including housing and financial problems) is revealed.

In general, there is an overrepresentation in the centers of the parts of the population who have few resources and can be said to suffer from the current economic crisis. In the self-help groups in Århus, in 1990, 11 percent of the clients were enrolled in some kind of educational program, 42 percent were employed, and 47 percent were supported by the public welfare system (that is, they were unemployed, elderly, or disabled) (Elgaard, 1990). There is also a striking correlation among unemployment of both women and men, perceived economic problems in the family, and the cases of violence and abuse of women, as shown in the statistics from the crises centers (Århus Kommune, 1983; Frederiksværk, 1990; Odense, 1990). Similarly, only about 33 percent of those who contact the advisory centers have employment income (Hansen, Hansen, Topsøe-Jensen, & Willert, 1991).

Institutionalization

All of the centers started more or less as a part of a grassroots movement (that is, the women's movement), having a very loose and volunteer-based organizational structure. They are all associations with general assemblies and elected boards, but they differ in the way in which they handle nationwide coordination, the autonomy of the centers, and daily management.

The advisory and crises centers have been gradually institutionalized both with regard to the organization and the financing since their start. The self-help centers have a less institutionalized way of dealing with their problems. For all the centers there is one central external force, namely the politicians, but the external coalition is not dominant in the sense that it seeks to influence the overall policy or the daily work of the associations. Because the associations are volunteer based, their internal coalitions are largely formed as the result of initiatives by individuals and groups of individuals. The advisory centers are the only centers that have had a permanently divided internal coalition and major political conflicts.

After they began in 1983, when everything was dealt with on an ad hoc and voluntary basis, the advisory centers soon developed a structure in which all six centers throughout the country had the same organization with identical goals and statutes. The central authority is the elected board with its chairman, Hanne Reintoft, and the appointed manager situated in Copenhagen. In 1986, when the concept spread throughout the country, it became obvious that there were some serious inherent problems.

There are two intertwined lines of conflict, one between Copenhagen and the rest of the country and one between the chairperson and central management and the volunteers. The centers outside Copenhagen feel that decisions come from the center and that they are being left out. The volunteers also feel left out because decisions come from management; this is, of course, the core of the problem. The open conflict was triggered by a decision by the central board in Copenhagen to employ a manager in Århus without discussing this with the volunteers of the Århus affiliation. This decision represented a total violation of the guiding values and self-image of these centers as being a part of a democratically led and participatory-oriented grassroots movement. After a fruitless attempt by the volunteers to have a dialogue with the central board, and after they had been publicly accused of being troublemakers, alcoholics, and unfit for their work, the volunteers decided to leave the association; so did the "support association" (a group of people in the background providing moral support for the local center).

In reaction the central board decided that from that point on, every volunteer would have to commit himself or herself to be loyal to the association, that the support association of the advisory centers should not be allowed to have quarters within the centers, and that every center should have an employed manager appointed directly by the central board in

Copenhagen. Unfortunately, this episode is not unique. There have been a number of similar incidents in which people left the association or have been dismissed because they would not and could not cooperate with the central management, notably Hanne Reintoft. The conflict seems rooted in disputes over managerial performance, not in ideology or ambiguity concerning means and ends. The latter type of conflicting interests can be interpreted as a strength (Pahl, 1979), whereas the conflicts in this case cannot. The way in which these incidents have been resolved has always been the same. Ultimate and authoritative decisions have been taken and executed from the top down. The managers and volunteers, when refusing to be overruled by the central board, have been accused of being disloyal, rebellious, and unfit for their work and have been replaced by others.

At present, the situation seems to have stabilized; the newly appointed managers are loyal to the central board, and new volunteers seem to be joining the advisory centers. Most of the centers have regular, local meetings to which all employees and voluntary personnel are invited, but because not all people attend all meetings, many decisions are in practice made by the manager.

Taking the advisory center in Århus as an example, the manager works closely with the secretary on certain practical decisions, often discussed in the morning. Once a week there is a meeting to coordinate efforts and to discuss principal decisions in which the advisers, the secretary, and the volunteers participate. However, many of the volunteers do not come to these weekly meetings, but most of them are present at the meeting that takes place once a month. The monthly meeting has no decision authority, so it is not a total democracy; all the important decisions are made at the weekly meeting, and the manager has ultimate responsibility. The way in which these centers function can probably best be understood against the background of the professional culture guiding their daily work. All of the advisory centers have a number of full-time employees, mostly social advisers, but there are also doctors, lawyers, and psychologists as part-time employees. The dominant culture is one in which mutuality, cooperation, and joint decision making are essential. This is reflected by the fact that there are no closed meetings.

Altogether the concept of the advisory centers and their methods of treatment are much the same throughout the country; this stabilization and standardization can partly be explained as the outcome of the political processes for which Hanne Reintoft has succeeded in gaining support and the fact that after 1989 the advisory centers succeeded in securing themselves financial support of 4 million kroner annually from the state budget (amounting to about 40 percent of the annual budget of each center), a successful strategic use of political co-optation and economic "piggybacking" (Galbraith, 1977; R. P. Nielsen, 1986). The co-optation strategy succeeded because the political legitimacy was established by positive public image making, by gaining access to political institutions, and by incorporating central political figures in the board. The piggy-backing strategy enabled the centers to use funds (the 4 million kroner) that were initially meant for educational activities to administer and run core activities of the centers.

The crises centers are less homogeneous than the advisory centers. Each of them has its own profile, and they are not centrally coordinated like the advisory centers. The crises centers have become highly institutionalized, both because they have a high percentage of staff employees (two of the seven centers examined have no volunteers attached) with fixed rules and working procedures and because all of them are totally dependent on public support either through grants from or contracts with the local authorities. The central authority is the elected board of each center. Some of the centers, however, emphasize their decentralized structure by making all important decisions (including those concerning money) at weekly meetings where all employees are present and by delegating administrative authority in all day-to-day matters (Odense, 1990).

Some of the meetings at these centers are regarded as house meetings in which all members of the crises center association, including the board, employees, and clients, are present. However, this reminiscence from the activist past of the centers has caused some trouble because the statutes of the centers, which define the centers as both self-governing institutions and as institutions whose boards are the ultimate authority, seem to collide. During the start-up phase of the center in Århus, there was a contradiction within the same paragraph of the statute, with one sentence reading that the "common meeting" of the association should decide on decisive questions concerning the way in which the center was run and another sentence reading that the common meeting cannot make decisions that are not in accord with decisions made previously by the board (Århus Kommune, 1983). If the center is to be governed in accordance with the contract with the local authorities (and the center is now on contract with the local authorities), there cannot be such a thing as a democratic assembly that is responsible for decision making. There is a dilemma between the guiding values of the centers, which emphasize that mutuality and participation in as many processes as possible is a part of the treatment, and the external expectations thrust on the centers as paragovernmental institutions.

Self-help centers and groups are more ad hoc based with fewer work procedures than the advisory or crisis centers. Basically, self-help centers are associations with a general assembly and an elected board responsible for the activities. The board also decides on the general policy, and members of the board have contact with the political system. The board members are also active as volunteers both in the groups and with administrative duties, with board members each often donating between 30 and 40 hours a month.

The self-help centers are also less institutionalized than the other two types of centers. They are less economically dependent on public support, and the organizational structure is less formalized. The daily work in the groups is less dependent economically on external funding because the main resource is the volunteers and the engagement of the participants in the groups. This loose network of groups is held together by the central administrative and coordinating office and the one or two persons employed there. The job of the employed coordinator is to give the volunteers a two-day introduction to group dynamics (for example, how to initiate without manipulating) and to evaluate, choose, and assign volunteers to a self-help group. Furthermore, the coordinator is responsible for the creation of new groups with new topics if needed, for the composition of each group (members of the groups are chosen through intensive interviews and conversations over the telephone or in the office), and for most of the external activities (for example, making speeches, contacting newspapers, and raising funds).

The self-help centers throughout the country consult each other from time to time to provide support and discuss common problems. However, these meetings have no central authority; each center has total autonomy.

Like the other centers, the self-help centers depend on public support to pay for the manager's salary and facility space. However, this local economic support is on a yearly basis, and there is no guarantee that the money will be awarded the following year.

This is a paradox considering the amount of voluntary effort that is put into the self-help groups. In 1991 there were 72 volunteers. In addition, the board puts in approximately 245 hours of voluntary work per month. The annual budget is 375,000 kroner, of which 250,000 kroner is the salary of the coordinator (Elgaard, 1990). Of the 375,000 kroner annual budget, 180,000 kroner is a donation from the local government of Århus, an additional 180,000 kroner is given by Århus County, and the rest is derived from membership fees, donations, and income from educational classes. It should be noted that the center pays only a symbolic rent for its office space and for the numerous private and public facilities that the self-help groups use. Vibeke Elgaard, the present coordinator, estimates the annual cost of each self-help group to be approximately 5,000 kroner—an inexpensive way of handling severe social problems.

Volunteers

There is a relatively large number of volunteers in all sections of the advisory centers, and the distribution is relatively homogeneous (the ratio between employees and volunteers is 1:4), whereas there are either no or many volunteers in each crises center. Furthermore, the volunteers seem to work more frequently in the advisory centers than in the crises centers. However, volunteers work equally as long in both places, on average from two to six hours a week.

The general opinion in the advisory centers is that they have plenty of volunteers, whereas the crises centers could use more volunteers (apart, of course, from the two centers who have and want none). This impression is strengthened by the fact that there has been a reduction in the number of volunteers in the crises centers over the past few years, whereas the advisory centers have witnessed stability and even increases in their number of volunteers. The self-help centers have no problem finding volunteers; their problem is choosing the right people for the job.

For the crises centers, getting enough volunteers is becoming critical as the number of clients increases and their cases become more severe. Some of the crises centers have tried to compensate for the increased client base by hiring more employees and by asking current volunteers to work harder. The lack of volunteers may explain why there are more external activities (for example, campaigns, advertising, meetings, and other informational activity) in crises centers than in the advisory centers. In crises centers, additional volunteers would prove a critical resource.

It is interesting to note that none of the managers in any of the centers has any managerial education, but they are professional in that they are experienced in the work that has to be done concerning the clients. Whereas the employed staff mostly consist of social advisors, the volunteers have a more diverse background. However, almost all of them are professionally engaged within the social and health sectors in their daily work as social advisers, psychologists, physicians, nurses, midwives, teachers, and lawyers. This diverse composition of the volunteers probably accounts for the good relationship between the public and the voluntary nonprofit system (they know each other and the system). There are few students, and only a few of the volunteers have as their primary qualification that they themselves have been victims. There are some people, especially in the self-help groups and the crises centers, who act as volunteers and help others from their own experience, but this is not the rule.

Public funding of the self-help centers is minimal. The volunteers truly are the critical resource, and the ratio between the direct economic investment of the public system and the voluntary contribution is more favorable here than in any of the other centers. The basic principle of these groups is that the participants be active in the process—this truly is help to self-help. Most of the volunteers are professionals in that they have a background in social work, and this is true of the board members as well. People are not engaged because of their management or political skills, and these organizations are not made up of depend on "charity ladies." Volunteers are interviewed and have to pass an educational course; if the coordinator finds a fit, they can be assigned to a group.

Differences and Similarities among the Centers

Even if there are some methodological reservations as to the representativeness of the survey, the general picture presented of the characteristic differences among the types of centers is probably realistic. The economic expenditure per client is about 1,200 kroner (about $200) in the advisory centers, between 4,000 and 7,000 kroner (about $1,000) in the crises centers, and about 600 kroner ($100) in the self-help centers, and there are regional disparities (for example, the self-help groups in Copenhagen are more expensive than the ones in Århus).

It is interesting to find that these differences are also reflected in the ratio of workers (employees and volunteers) to client: more than 1:1 in the crises centers and less than 1:1 in the advisory centers and the self-help centers. This picture becomes even more distinctive if one looks at the amount of time spent by employees and volunteers on each client: between two and nine hours per client in the advisory centers and between 20 and 30 hours per client in the crises centers. These figures are a bit difficult to calculate for the self-help centers, but the time spent per client is probably low because each volunteer does not attend to one person but rather to a whole group at a time.

There are distinctive differences among the three types of centers for women, and these differences clearly reflect the field of work, the clients, and the working conditions of each type of center. The crises centers are the most expensive to run, and they have the heaviest workload. This is only natural, however, because they have to be open both day and night and some clients stay for several days. Handling social problems always tends to involve vast amounts of human work; that is why voluntary-based initiatives have a comparative advantage over those public and private institutions that have to pay all their employees.

Mutual Dependence and Alternative and Supplementary Services

The relationship between the centers and public authorities has two primary aspects: (1) funding of the centers and (2) referral by and to the centers. Public funding is vital to all the centers. Given the minimal public funding, volunteers are a critical resource in all centers but two. However, it is essential to have both the economic aid and the facilities that public authorities can provide. For some of the centers, this public support seems to have been stabilized. This is certainly the case for the crises centers that are on contract with local authorities. It is also the case for the advisory centers that get a considerable amount of their funding from the state budget and state redistribution of lottery funds. Nevertheless, this public funding for the advisory centers is on a year-to-year basis, and this puts a considerable constraint on the centers and increases their unease with an uncertain future. The self-help centers face even greater uncertainty and survive from year to year on the goodwill of the politicians. They have difficulty finding other external funding sources because it is hard to make private foundations pay for the daily costs (mostly the salary of the coordinator) that constitute the bulk of the budget.

Aside from economic dependency, cooperation among the centers and between them and the public authorities stems from the practice of dealing with the same customers and clients and referring them to the other centers. Centers send clients to one another if they discover that the client's problem is not within the scope of their expertise. In this way, there is no competition among the centers; they supplement each other and share the market—clients may need to go concurrently to more than one center. The reason for this cooperation is probably twofold: (1) The centers are alternatives to each other and money only indirectly follows the customers (the need for support is indicated by yearly figures of the number of clients) and (2) the managers are not formally educated managers who might think in competitive terms (that is, expansion of market shares and related diversification) but professionals. Basically, these centers and the public authorities have the same interest; their professional organizational culture is the same, and they all function within the negotiated economy.

The relationship between the centers and the public authorities again is one of mutuality. The self-help centers often get their customers by reference from public authorities and from the other centers; most of their clients, however, come because they have heard of the initiative or read about it in the newspapers (the centers advertise their open groups). The crises centers receive clients who have been advised to apply to them for help by the police and by the social security system, and the advisory centers receive clients from the social security system and from physicians, lawyers, and midwives.

In general, the relationship with public authorities is perceived as good by all the centers. The public financial support and the fact that public authorities have a seat on some of the boards of the associations on contract with them is not perceived as a constraint to the way in which centers may act. Far from being scrutinized by public authorities, many of the centers view themselves as the public scrutinizer (that is, they make sure that their clients are being treated fairly by public authorities and advise them of their rights). The advisory centers primarily consider themselves alternatives to public service, whereas the crises centers and self-help groups primarily consider themselves as supplementary to public services.

Even if the advisory centers may be looked on as alternatives insofar as they provide the same services to the same groups of people, they also supplement the public system. The public system refers clients to the advisory centers for their specialized expertise based on the center's mission, focus, and methods as well as the organizational climate and culture in which the service is offered.

The advisory centers (and to a large extent the crises centers and self-help groups) do not have to register and make a file on each person who contacts them. This flexibility motivates clients to go to these centers instead of the public authorities. People are often afraid that a registration of their problems may be compiled with other data on them and used against them. There are special situations when this sort of information may be considered vitally important (for example, when public authorities have to decide whether parents are fit to look after their own children). In addition, the physical surroundings are not institution-like (but often rather old and worn out), and the social atmosphere is more personal and intimate, often based on an atmosphere of mutual trust that develops because there is nothing to fear and clients feel that the volunteers may have had similar experiences.

The crises centers are primarily a supplement to the public system because they deliver services that public agencies do not provide. They can handle acute crises, are open around the clock and on weekends and holidays, and allow clients to stay there for several days. The crises that people experience have to be very dramatic or severe before the public institutions that are open around the clock accept them. And hospitals, police stations, and psychiatric hospitals are not places where people would like to spend the night, let alone several days. (It would not cost clients anything to use these services, but these are places people go when they are either seriously ill or very threatened.) Because many of the crises centers are on contract with and totally financed by public authorities, it is likely that they are looked on by the authorities as supplementary or even as a part of the public system.

The self-help groups are primarily looked on as a supplement to public services because there are no similar public activities and because the work of the self-help groups can be regarded neither as treatment nor as counseling; the groups initiate activities and help to create social networks. The self-help groups, however, may function as a relief to public agencies both preventively and as a follow-up when people leave public institutions. Because the participants in the self-help groups are characterized by their relatively weak personal and social networks, it is possible to argue that these groups may function as a kind of substitute or supplement to civil society inasmuch as it is manifested in family, friends, and social networks.

Overall, the relationship among the centers and between them and the public authorities is characterized by their mutual dependency; each of them refers clients to the others. Furthermore, the centers depend on public funding. The mutual dependence is most pronounced when it comes to the crises centers, a little less pronounced in the case of the advisory centers, and least evident in the self-help groups. In other words, the self-help groups depend more on public authorities than public authorities do on them. Or maybe it just seems to be so because it is easier to recognize and argue that the other two types of centers are relieving public authorities from the responsibility of dealing with these clients, whereas in the case of the self-help groups, this is only shown in the long run.

The present state of the mutual relationships may help explain both the more or less stable situation and economic funding of the centers and their relative institutionalization. The character of the mutual relationships may be key to understanding not only their interaction with each other, but also their individual organizational behavior—their processes of institutionalization.

Of the three types of paragovernmental institutions, the crises centers are the most highly institutionalized nongovernmental providers of public services. Some centers are totally integrated into the public system as self-governing institutions, and only some have retained their dependency on volunteers. The advisory centers are also highly institutionalized providers of alternative services, yet they are still economically vulnerable and depend heavily on volunteers. The self-help groups are less institutionalized and less integrated within the public system, economically insecure, and totally dependent on volunteers.

Current Managerial Situation

If we look at the current situation of the centers, their environment and future development seem fairly predictable. With the present social situation, it is unlikely that the centers will run out of clients in the foreseeable future and, with the general political goodwill the centers enjoy and the established relationship already in place with the public system, it is unlikely that they should not be allowed to continue their work. However, this does not mean that their future—like their current—existence is without problems.

At present, there are relatively good working conditions in the centers, without too many disputes and conflicting interests (apart maybe from the relationship between some of the advisory centers and their central management); the centers need a larger capacity; and the centers, especially the self-help groups, probably wish for more steady and secure funding (apart from two of the crises centers that are on contract with local authorities).

Because money does not follow people and there is both a geographic and service specialization among the centers, there is no competition but rather a clear division of labor and cooperation among the centers and between them and the public authorities. Although the target groups for each center are differentiated because of the division of work and specialization of services, they may be looked on as relatively homogeneous. Finally, the current problems of the centers are relatively complex and require highly skilled expertise and large amounts of time and patience.

In Mintzberg's (1983) terminology, the centers all resemble the simple structure, often with one central leading figure, yet still very much in line with the democratic tradition of the association. In the case of the advisory centers, this structure is combined with a high degree of centralization of decision authority and the unification of goals and working procedures. The crises centers have been heavily influenced by the institutionalization and professional bureaucratization of working procedures, whereas in the self-help groups everything is dealt with on a more ad hoc basis and with a large autonomy of each of the groups.

According to Handy's (1988) distinctions among four ideal types of organizational culture, the centers seem close to all four types in different ways and on different dimensions. The political process between the advisory centers and the central management in Copenhagen is part of a "power culture" in which the important issues are dealt with closely or in line with the wishes of Hanne Reintoft. The working conditions of the crises centers are similar to a "role culture," particularly a "task culture" in which the guiding principles are linked to the cases and to the expertise and the rules of the professionals. The role of the individuals in the self-help groups is part of an "individualized culture" in which the development of each group greatly depends on the initiatives of each volunteer and the participation of all group members.

An analysis of the centers in relationship to Handy's distinctions accounts for the way in which conflicts are resolved in the advisory centers and for their successful strategy of co-optation (gaining political support). Yet at the same time, this analysis illustrates the dependence of the centers on one central person and the need for more flexibility and decentralization if the association is not to lose its legitimacy. Furthermore, an analysis of this sort accounts for the high affinity between the crises centers and the public system and reveals the accountability, the capacity for dealing with difficult problems, and the inflexibility of such systems. The centers that are not on contract with public authorities probably should put more emphasis on their external activities to gain political and economic support and to attract more volunteers. Much the same can be said about the self-help groups, which continue to operate on a day-to-day (or year-to-year) basis. Although both the board members and the daily manager of these centers have tried to develop stronger external relationships, they have thus far only been able to secure the immediate future of the groups. The individualized culture of the self-help groups may help to explain the relative strength of systems in which those who take initiatives are setting the pace; yet at the same time, the culture reveals the vulnerability of the self-help groups if their central coordinative unit should fail (that is, not succeed in gaining funding).

So far, the strategic focus of these centers has been neither the bottom line (as in private firms) nor political legitimacy (as in public organizations); the strategic focus is on the development of services and the relationships with the clients (that is, the evaluation criteria depend on professional ethical norms and values). All the centers reveal some kind of cooperative strategy (Galbraith, 1977; R. P. Nielsen, 1988), which is only natural because there is no direct competition. On the contrary, there is an indirect as well as a direct division of the market. Some centers more than others deliberately seek influence on public decision making and try to incorporate important persons from the task environment into their boards (co-optation strategies), and contracts are widely used.

Future Managerial Strategies

Various cooperative strategies could probably be applied more successfully if managers and board members had the time and skills to do so. It should be noted again that none of the managers has any formal managerial education—they are all social workers. This has its advantages in the internal processes of the organizations and in the match of cultures with the professional system of public authorities. However, it also has a limiting effect on external relations (that is, strategic management). And, because of the lack of managerial experience, there is no deliberate strategy (with one exception) to include persons on the board who have finance, accounting, or political decision-making skills or connections.

From a public relations perspective, the centers should place more emphasis on their comparative advantages—the fact that they engage volunteers and provide low-cost services. In Galbraith's terminology (1977), this would be a "voluntary response" strategy—an independent rather than a cooperative strategy. However, current strategy formation is largely ad hoc and strategic management is nonexistent. Although the centers may conceive of strategies such as cooperation, co-optation, and economic piggybacking, strategic management as applied in textbooks and management theory in general (Johnson & Scholes, 1988; Porter, 1980) and regarding nonprofits in particular (Espy, 1986; Hatten, 1982; McLaughlin, 1986; R. P. Nielsen 1986), are alien concepts in these small voluntary organizations (Klausen, 1990). The strategies of these centers evolve incrementally. None of the associations analyzed here practice organizational development or strategic management in the sense in which it is usually practiced. Where there are management ambitions (for example, in the central management of the advisory centers), these initiatives seem to be utterly out of line with both the image and the guiding values of voluntary associations. Management in the centers is very much a matter of everyday administration and survival.

Summing Up the Perspective

The development of the welfare state beginning in the 1930s may be seen in accordance with the deliberate policy of many voluntary associations. In this sense both the institutionalization of the associations and the creation of the welfare state may be seen not as the imperialistic usurpation of these organizations by the state (that is, not as the colonization of the life world by the systems world), but rather the other way around (Klausen, 1989). The way in which the centers for women discussed here have been integrated into the public system as paragovernmental institutions demonstrates how the welfare state can adapt to new situations; it also shows how these centers have been able to integrate themselves into the modern negotiated economy. In a larger historical perspective, this process of adaptation is in line with the peaceful historical heritage and the collective and solidaristic values guiding Danish society in general.

Today, totally independent voluntary nonprofit institutions play only a minor role in the provision of social services in Denmark. But if all the voluntary associations and private nonprofit self-governing institutions that are either highly economically dependent on public support or on contract with public authorities are included, they do play a role in providing services to special groups (as is the case with the advisory and crises centers and self-help groups) and become an important part or extension of the welfare state. Almost all of the centers for women have people on waiting lists, which demonstrates their limited capacity and the need for more support for the centers.

The organizations that have been discussed here began operating on the fringe of society because they were dealing with controversial problems and because they operated within a radical ideological framework that emphasized that problems women were facing were connected with class struggle and the struggle for women's rights. They have not only helped numerous women but also have achieved a role as a social innovative force. The problems of women have not only been identified, they have been recognized as a public responsibility. This recognition accounts for the development of mutual dependency in which these associations have been more or less institutionalized within the realm of the public system. However, even if these centers are viewed as a paragovernmental way of dealing with specific social problems, the way in which they do so allows them to remain different from public institutions. This is precisely why they are considered both alternative and supplementary to the public social services system. The overall organizational development of these groups is one of institutionalization and professionalism. The centers are concentrating on the development of specialized expertise. The identity of those people attached to the centers have to a large extent shifted away from the ideological and political aspects of the women's movement toward specific problems of individual clients; the focus is now on professional service and high ethical standards.

These private voluntary and nonprofit centers are not the revival or the introduction of the "residual welfare model" inasmuch as this model is "based on the premise that there are two 'natural' (or socially given) channels through which an individual's needs are properly met; the private market and the family" (Titmuss, 1974, p. 30). The centers may be seen as an extension and integrated part of the public welfare system, a part of the "institutional model," allowing for selective discrimination.

References

Århus Kommune. (1983). *Krisecentret for voldsramte kvinder i Århus. Delrapport II [The crisis center for battered women. Report II].* Århus: Author.

Budgetdepartementet Udgiftsanalyser. (1990). *De offentlige udgifters vækst og fordeling [The growth and distribution of public expenses].* Copenhagen: Budgetdepartementet, Finansministeriet.

Buksti, J., & Johansen, L. N. (1979). Organisationssystemet i Danmark [The organizational system in Denmark]. In M. N. Pedersen (Ed.), *Dansk politik i 1970'erne—studier og arbejds papirer [Danish politics in the 1970s—studies and working papers]* (pp. 223–263). Århus: Samfundsvidenskabeligt Forlag.

Christensen, J. (1988). National report: Denmark. In T. Modeen & A. Rosas (Eds.), *Indirect public administration in fourteen countries* (pp. 65–85). Åbo: Åbo Academy Press.

Danmarks Statistik [Central Bureau of Statistics]. (1991). *Nyt fra Danmarks Statistik* nr. 314. Copenhagen: Danmarks Statistik.

Elgaard, V. (1990). *Beskrivelse af Selvhjælpsgrupperne i Århus, [A description of the self-help groups in Århus]*. Århus: Selvhjælp sgrupperne: Århus.

Engelstoft, P., & Jensen, H. (Eds.). (1930). *Sociale studier i dansk historie efter 1857 [Social studies of Danish history after 1857]*. Copenhagen: Institut for historie og samfundsøkonomi.

Ericson, R., Hansen E. J., Ringen, S., & Uusitalo, H. (Eds.). (1987). *The Scandinavian model*. New York: M. E. Sharpe.

Espy, S. N. (1986). *Handbook of strategic planning for nonprofit organizations*. New York: Praeger.

Flensted-Jensen, E., Frastein, S., & Pedersen, A. S. (1977). *Mellem opgør og tilpasning. Kvindebevægelsen og kvindesituationen i Danmark siden - 68 [Between confrontation and adjustment. Women's liberation and women's situation in Denmark since '68]* (Vol. 1, No. 2). Århus: Modtryk.

Flora, P. (1986). *Growth to limits* (Vol. 4). Berlin: Walter de Guyter.

Frederiksværk. (1990). *Krisecentret i Frederiksværk. Årsberetning for 1990 [The crises center in Frederiksværk]*. Frederiksvaerk: Krisecentret i Frederiksværk.

Fyns Amts Krisecenter. (1990). *Fyns amts krisecenter for voldsramte kvinder. Årsberetning 1990 [Crisis center for battered women in the county of Funen. Annual Report 1990]*. Odense, Denmark: Fyns Amts.

Galbraith, J. (1977). *Organization design*. London: Addison-Wesley.

Giese, S. (1973). *Derfor kvindekamp [Hence women's lib struggle]*. Copenhagen: Tiderne Skifter.

Habermann, U. (1987). *Det tredie netvaerk—en grundbog om frivilligt arbejde [The third network—an introduction to voluntary work]*. Copenhagen: Akademisk Forlag.

Handy, C. B. (1988). *Understanding voluntary organizations*. New York: Penguin Books.

Hansen, F. K., Hansen H., Topsøe-Jensen, H., & Willert, H. (1991). *Mødrehjælpens klienter og aktiviteter [Clients and activities of advisory centers]*. Copenhagen: Center for Alternativ Samfundsanalyse.

Hansen, H. (1930). Den nye drøftelse af sociale spørgsmaal 1890–94. [The new discussion of social questions 1890–94]. In P. Engelstoft &

H. Jensen, (Eds.) *Sociale studier i dansk historie efter 1857 [Social studies of Danish history after 1857]* (pp. 128–148). *Copenhagen*.

Hatten, M. L. (1982). Strategic management in not-for-profit organizations. *Strategic Management Journal, 3*, 89–104.

Hernes, G. (Ed.). (1985). *Forhandlingsøkonomi og blandingsadministrasjon [Negotiated economy and mixed administration]*. Oslo: Universitetsforlaget.

Hood, C., & Schuppert, G. F. (Eds.). (1988). *Delivering public services in western Europe. Sharing western European experience on para-government organization*. London: Sage Publications.

Johansen, L. N., & Kolberg, J. E. (1985). Welfare state regression in Scandinavia? The development of the Scandinavian welfare state from 1970 to 1980. In S. N. Eisentadt & O. Ahimeir (Eds.), *The welfare state and its aftermath* (pp. 143–176). London: Croom Helm.

Johnson, G., & Scholes, K. (1988). *Exploring corporate strategy*. Englewood Cliffs, NJ: Prentice Hall.

Klausen, K. K. (1982). *Komparativ revolutionsforskning. De borgerlige revolutioner [Comparative revolution research. Bourgeois revolution]*. Unpublished master's thesis, Århus Universitet, Århus, Denmark.

Klausen, K. K. (1986). Industrielle konflikter [Industrial conflicts]. In F. Mikkelsen (Ed.), *Protest og oprør. Kollektive aktioner i Danmark 1700–1985 [Protest and revolt. Collective action in Denmark 1700–1985]* (pp. 132–167). Århus: Modtryk.

Klausen, K. K. (1989). Den tredje sektor. Frivillige organisationer mellem stat og marked [Voluntary organizations between state and market]. In K. K. Klausen & T. H. Nielsen (Ed.), *Stat og marked. Fra Leviathan og usynlig hånd til forhandlingsøkonomi [State and market. From Leviathan and invisible hand to negotiated economy]* (pp. 227–282). Charlottenlund: Jurist-og Økonomforbundets Forlag.

Klausen, K. K. (1990). *Organisatorisk inerti og mikrodynamiske processer. Ledelsesmæssige og organisatoriske processer i frivillige organisationer [Organizational inertia and microdynamic processes. Leadership and organizational processes in voluntary organizations]*. Copenhagen: Samfundslitteratur.

Klausen, K. K. (1991). Private welfare provision. In T. Knudsen (Ed.), *Welfare administration in Denmark* (pp. 243–270). Copenhagen: Ministry of Finance.

Klausen, K. K. (1992). *Paragovernmental organizations, the extension of the welfare state—Voluntary and nonprofit centers for women in Denmark* (Political Science Publication). Odense: Odense University, Department of Political Science.

Klausen, K. K., & Evertsen, A. (1992). *Alternativ velfærdsproduktion? Rapport om rådgivnings- og krisecentre for kvinder [Alternative welfare production? Report on advisory and crisis centers for women]*. (Political Science Publication). Odense: Odense University, Department of Commercial Law and Political Science.

Klausen, K. K., & Mikkelsen, F. (1988). *Konflikter, kollektive aktioner og protestbevægelser i Danmark [Conflicts, collective actions, and protest movements in Denmark]*. Silkeborg: Samfundsfagsnyt.

Kramer, R. (1981). *Voluntary agencies in the welfare state*. Berkeley: University of California Press.

Kuhnle, S. (1989). Den skandinaviske velferdsmodell. Skandinavisk? Velferd? Modell? [The Scandinavian welfare model. Scandinavian? Welfare? Model?]. In A. Hovdum, et al. (Eds.), V*isjoner om velferdssamfunnet [Visions of the welfare society]* (pp. 12–20). Bergen: Alma Mater Forlag As.

Kuhnle, S., & Selle, P. (1990). Innledning: Frivillige organisasjoner og den tredje sektor [Introduction: Voluntary organizations and the third sector]. In S. Kuhnle, & P. Selle (Eds.), *Frivillig organisert velferd—Alternativ til Offentlig? [Voluntarily organized welfare—An alternative to public welfare?]* (pp. 9–28). Bergen: Alma Mater Forlag As.

Kuhnle, S., & Solheim, L. (1985). *Velferdsstaten—Vekst og omstilling [The welfare state—Growth and readjustment]*. Oslo: TANO.

Madsen, A. B. (1986). Kvindekamp og kollektive aktioner omkring århundredeskiftet [Women's lib struggle and collective actions around the turn of the century]. In F. Mikkelsen (Ed.), *Protest og oprør [Protest and rebellion]* (pp. 169–192). Viborg: Modtryk.

McLaughlin C. P. (Ed.). (1986). *The management of nonprofit organizations*. New York: John Wiley & Sons.

Mintzberg, H. (1983). *Structures in fives: Designing effective organizations*. Englewood Cliffs, NJ: Prentice Hall.

Nielsen, K., & Pedersen, O. K. (Eds.). (1989a). *Forhandlingsøkonomi i Norden [Negotiated economy in Nordic countries]*. Charlottenlund: Jurist- og Økonomforbundets Forlag.

Nielsen, K., & Pedersen, O. K. (1989b). Fra blandingsøkonomi til forhandlingsøkonomi. Mod et nyt paradigme? [From mixed economy to negotiated economy. Toward a new paradigm?]. In K. K. Klausen & T. H. Nielsen (Eds.), *Stat og marked. Fra Leviathan og usynlig hånd til forhandlingsøkonomi [State and market. From Leviathan and invisible hand to negotiated economy]* (pp. 171–226). Charlottenlund: Jurist- og Økonomforbundets Forlag.

Nielsen, R. P. (1986). Piggybacking strategies for nonprofits: A shared costs approach. *Strategic Management Journal, 7*, 201–215.

Nielsen, R. P. (1988). Cooperative strategy. *Strategic Management Journal, 9*, 475–492.

Nordic Statistical Secretariat (Ed.) (1986/1987). *Yearbook of Nordic Statistics*. Stockholm: Nordic Council of Ministers.

Nørregaard, G. (1930). *Arbejderspørgsmaalet i Firserne [The labor question in the eighties]*. In P. Engelstoft & H. Jensen (Eds.), *Sociale studier i dansk historie efter 1857 [Social studies of Danish history after 1857]* (pp. 100–127). Copenhagen: Institut for historie og Samfundsø Konomi.

Nørregaard, G. (1943). *Arbejdsforhold indenfor dansk haandværk of industri 1857–1899 [Working conditions in Danish trade and industry, 1857–1899]*. Copenhagen: Gyldendal og Nordisk Forlag.

Pahl, J. (1979). Refuges for battered women: Social provision or social movement? *Journal of Voluntary Action Research, 8*(1–2), 25–35.

Parsby, I. (1988). *Forsvinder de selvejende institutioner? En undersøgelse af udviklingen i antallet af selvejende og offentlige institutionspladser 1980–1986. [Are self-governing institutions disappearing? An analysis of the development in the number of self-governing and public institutions, 1980–1986]*. Copenhagen: Kontaktudvalget.

Pedersen, O. K. (1988). Den sønderdelte stat. Om interesse-organisationernes integration i den offentlige forvaltning og effekterne heraf [The divided state. On the integration of interest organizations in the public sector and its effects]. *Statsvidenskabelig Tidskrift, 3*, 259–278.

Porter, M. E. (1980). *Competitive strategy: Techniques for analyzing industries and competitors*. New York: Free Press.

Rose, R. (1986). Common goals but different roles: The state's contribution to the welfare mix. In R. Rose & R. Shatori (Eds.), *The welfare state east & west* (pp. 13–39). New York: Oxford University Press.

Statistisk Oversigt. (1992). Levevilkår i *Danmark statistisk oversigt 1992 [Living conditions in Denmark statistical survey]*. Copenhagen: Danmarks Statistik, Socialforskningsinstituttet.

Titmuss, R. (1974). S*ocial policy.* London: Allen & Unwin.

Togeby, L. & Svensson, P. (1991). *Højrebølgen? [The right wing wave?].* Århus: Politica.

Warmdahl, G. (1930). Statens Stilling til Arbejderspørgsmaalet i halvfjerdserne. Arbejderkommissionen af 1875 [The attitude of the state to the labor question in the seventies. The Labour Commission of 1875]. In P. Engelstoft & H. Jensen (Eds.) *Sociale Studier i dansk historie efter 1857 [Social studies of Danish history after 1857]* (pp. 64–81). Copenhagen: Institut for historie og samfundsøkonomi.

Wilensky, H., & Libeaux, C. N. *Industrial society and social welfare*. New York: Russell Sage Foundation.

CHAPTER SIX

Israel

The Counseling Center for Women

Joseph Katan and Simi Mizrahi

This chapter describes and analyzes The Counseling Center for Women—an alternative feminist organization established in Israel in 1986. The center was established by a group of women in the human services professions who were highly skeptical of the ability of existing therapeutic services to provide proper assistance to women and who believed that only a new organization, guided by female perspectives, could adequately cope with the psychological problems of Israeli women.

The first part describes several major characteristics of the Israeli sociopolitical context and examines their possible relevance to the emergence and development of alternative organizations (AOs) in Israel. The second part reviews the structure of the Israeli welfare system and the role played in it by AOs. The third through seventh parts are devoted to description and analysis of the background, aims, approaches, structure, and activities of the center, as well as of its links with other organizations and its financial resources. The remaining sections of the chapter analyze the financial situation at the center at this stage of its development and consider its future development as an AO.

Sociopolitical Context

Since its establishment in 1948, Israel has been characterized by strong tendencies toward political and bureaucratic centralization, dominance of central organizations and political parties, hegemony of national leaders, and consensus among the majority of the Jewish population (which constitutes about 82 percent of the total population) on key values and political and social issues. However, these tendencies have been accompanied by parallel—although weak—

trends toward decentralization, disagreement, and conflict (Eisenstadt, 1967, 1985). In fact, the same factors that push toward centralization and consensus also contain the seeds of diversity and alternative approaches. The main characteristics of this sociopolitical context and their impact on the emergence and development of AOs, including women's AOs, are described below.

First, from its inception, Israel has faced security problems stemming from its tense relations with its Arab neighbors. The continual sense of threat, aggravated by many instances of terrorism, has instilled in Israelis a strong trend toward centralization, national solidarity, and consensus. However, the unsettled security situation also has spurred the formation of organizations—most of them small—that oppose the national consensus. Some of them call for more active efforts, accompanied by significant concessions, to achieve peace, whereas others totally reject compromise. The recent agreement between Israel and the Palestinians and the continuing negotiations with Jordan, Lebanon, and Syria may change this situation in the future.

Second, a large portion of the Israeli Jewish population consists of immigrants who arrived from many countries and from different sociocultural backgrounds. Because most of the immigrants came without economic resources, their absorption depended almost completely on aid they received from government authorities. This situation fostered in the Israeli public the feeling that the government is responsible for solving economic and social problems and, consequently, strengthened the position of central bodies and weakened local and alternative initiatives. Furthermore, aware of the danger of divisions among immigrants of different ethnic backgrounds, the government developed institutions such as a unified educational system to serve as a force for national identification, integration, and consensus. However, these initiatives have not prevented the formation of many ethnic organizations that wish to maintain the specific cultural heritage of their members and to represent their interests face-to-face with government authorities.

Third, the role of the Jewish religion in the state has similarly promoted both unity and diversity. Although the majority of Israeli Jews identify themselves as secular, they feel a strong attachment to Jewish tradition and agree that it must play a central role in the country. Indeed, religious norms have played a prominent role in Israel, especially in the areas of family life and women's status. There is no doubt that in an ethnically diverse country such as Israel the existence of a common religion fulfills a vital unifying and integrative function. However, the pivotal role of religion has provoked strong opposition among groups of secular Jews and women's organizations calling for the creation of a secular society free of religious intervention.

Fourth, the trends toward decentralization and pluralism that counterbalance to a certain degree the strong centralization processes are also related to the role played by voluntary organizations (VOs)—including several strong women's organizations—in the history of Israel. Prior to the establishment of the State in 1948, VOs played a major role in the organization of the Jewish community in Palestine and were active in almost every facet of life—from education, welfare, and housing to rural and urban development and defense. Some of these organizations, such as the kibbutzim (collective settlements), were characterized by the same equality, role rotation, and direct democracy espoused by AOs. When the State was established, some of these organizations were nationalized, especially in the areas of welfare, education, and defense. Nonetheless, the voluntary sector continued to act in many spheres, and in recent years it has even permeated new spheres of activity, often with government support.

This review of some of the major characteristics of the Israeli sociopolitical context suggests certain major factors that may promote or hinder the establishment and development of AOs in this country. These factors are briefly summarized in Table 1. Despite some new developments in recent years, the factors impeding the formation and growth of AOs still outweigh those that encourage them. Some of these hindering factors—especially the centralist trends and the strong tendency toward consensus—are particularly constraining the emergence and growth of women's AOs. Thus, even when women's AOs are established, they function in an environment that constrains their development and limits their impact.

Structure of Israel's Welfare System

The tendencies in Israeli society toward centralization and decentralization, unity and diversity, as well as the presence of factors that either promote or impede the foundation and development of AOs, are reflected in the structure and composition of the Israeli welfare system. This system includes a multitude of organizations and groups that belong to four main sectors: (1) the public (central government and local municipalities), (2) the voluntary (including AOs), (3) the private–commercial, and (4) the informal (Katan, 1990; Neipris, 1978). These sectors are briefly described below.

Public Sector
The central government plays a key role in the Israeli welfare system, directly supplying a wide range of social services, such as education and income maintenance, and financing many services delivered by other

Table 1
• •
Factors That Hinder and Promote the Formation of Alternative Organizations in Israel

HINDERING FACTORS	PROMOTING FACTORS
The centralist tendencies and the dominant role played by the political center	The gradual weakening of the legitimacy of the political center among parts of the public
The strong inclination toward social and political consensus	The pluralistic texture and the tradition of pluralism in Israeli society
The public conception that government is responsible for solving personal problems	The long-standing frustrations in Israeli society (absorption difficulties, discrimination against women, and so forth)
The wide range of services directly or indirectly provided by the government	
The impact of the religious dimension	The existence of AOs in Israel before the establishment of the State

• •

organizations. The central government operates in the welfare arena through several ministries, including the ministries of Labor and Social Affairs, Education and Culture, Health, Housing, and Immigrant Absorption. Another government body, the National Insurance Institute, is responsible for a wide range of income maintenance programs, including old age and survivor allowances, child allowances, maternity benefits, and unemployment insurance.

Municipal welfare departments assume direct responsibility for the delivery of most of the personal services. Although they vary in scope, diversity, and quality of activities, these departments generally provide a group of services that include consultation and treatment for individuals and families, referral of clients to other services, child welfare services, services for the elderly, rehabilitation services for the handicapped, and community organization activities.

Because most of the financial resources for these services are allocated by the Ministry of Labor and Social Affairs, this ministry guides and supervises the activities of the local departments. In addition, local governments also offer informal educational and psychological services to school children, and some governments have established public health departments that operate well-mother-and-child clinics.

Voluntary Sector

Voluntary organizations provide a wide range of services, many of them to individuals and families with disabled members. The government has transferred to VOs considerable responsibility for the delivery of services to segments of the population with serious physical, personal, and social handicaps. Some of these services are provided solely by VOs, whereas others also are offered by local welfare departments and private organizations. Child care is another area of service provided by VOs—mostly women's organizations.

Although the government views VOs as agencies for implementing segments of its social programs and finances a considerable part of their activities, VOs are by no means merely government agents. They function independently in areas where there is limited governmental involvement, and they often also fill the vacuum created by government cutbacks in social services and programs. A recent development in Israel is the rapid growth and proliferation of self-help organizations such as Alcoholics Anonymous and Narcotics Anonymous (Bargal & Gidron, 1983).

AOs operating in the welfare arena are a rare phenomenon, although in recent years several small organizations of this type providing services to women, gay men and lesbians, and other populations have emerged. Their number and impact are still very limited, however.

Commercial–Private Sector

The private sector has always operated in certain areas of welfare in Israel. Today its presence is especially marked in the health scene, although most health care is still provided by nonprofit sickness funds. This sector also plays a central role in delivering services to elderly people living in the community or in institutions, and in building houses for new immigrants, poor families, and young couples, also with government financial support.

Informal Sector

Informal support networks of relatives, neighbors, and friends are becoming an important component of human services. Several studies conducted in recent years on these networks in Israel indicate their special relevance to people who are aged and ill (Katan, 1989; Shmueli, Shoval, & Fleishman, 1983).

● ● ●

Israel is a pluralistic welfare state with a wide variety of organizations taking part in the delivery of services. The previous dominance of the central government in the provision of services has declined somewhat in recent years, but it continues to play a major part in financing and delivering a wide range of social services. Many services, however, are delivered by local governments, VOs, and private for-profit organizations. Several small AOs, founded in recent years, provide services to specific populations, but their influence is very limited. Although the various sectors and organizations just described provide services to needy populations, only a few of them provide services especially geared to the problems and needs of women.

Status, Problems, and Needs of Women in Israeli Society

Many observers perceive Israel as a state where women have successfully integrated into the mainstream of life and achieved a proper place in various spheres of activity. Among other things, Israel's appearance as an advanced western state, the fact that for several years a woman has served as prime minister, the conscription of women to army service, and the prominent role played by several women in the country's social and cultural lives have fostered this image.

However, Israel is also a state where women have unique problems, some of which are unknown in other western countries (Friedman, Izraeli, & Shrift, 1982; Lev-Ari, 1992).

- Marriage and divorce, so vital to people's lives, are regulated by religious authorities and laws that often discriminate against women. The rabbinic courts, which play a key role in implementing Israeli family law, consist only of men.

- Women's presence in influential political bodies is very marginal. Only about 10 percent of the Israeli cabinet and parliament members are women. Only one Israeli town has a woman mayor.

- Few women occupy high positions in the government bureaucracy or in industrial and commercial enterprises. Most women working in these frameworks occupy low-level positions.

- Despite legislation assuring equal rights to women and forbidding discrimination on the grounds of gender, there are still gaps between women's and men's salaries, even for the same work.

- Quite a few women (estimates of their number differ) suffer from physical abuse by husbands or boyfriends.

Over the years "conventional" women's VOs, such as Naamat (which belongs to the Federation of Israeli Trade Unions) and WIZO (International Organization of Jewish Zionist Women, committed to women's rights) have tried, with partial success, to improve the political and economic status of Israeli women by initiating equal rights legislation in several fields (such as equal salaries for men and women and equal access to employment opportunities) and by putting pressure on political parties to place more women in influential positions. But they have failed to repeal full religious control of family laws.

These conventional organizations have operated mainly through political parties and other bodies dominated by men and have used consensual tactics to achieve their objectives. Several attempts by active feminists to organize a women's party that would more rigorously fight discrimination against women failed. A women's party that ran in the last general election in June 1992, for example, received only a few hundred votes. Evidently, the large majority of Israeli women accept the consensual pattern of voting for male-dominated parties and reject separate women's political parties.

The conventional women's VOs were also active in developing and providing services designed at least partly to respond to women's needs. In fact, the central government regards these organizations as suitable to deliver services relevant to women, such a child care for mothers, family guidance, and social clubs. However, government financial support for these services is still limited. Women's organizations—some of them with a strong feminist orientation—also have played a pioneering role in raising public awareness of the problems of wife-battering, abuse, and rape. Some of these organizations have established shelters for battered women and their children, centers for counseling rape victims, and centers for prevention of domestic violence; however, only after these services were already established did the government provide partial financial support. These services tend to be small, however, so their ability to provide adequately for women's needs is limited.

The Counseling Center for Women was founded to meet a need that has not been met by other organizations: the provision of counseling services focusing on the specific psychological problems of Israeli women.

Establishment of the Center

In the view of the center's founders, women in Israel face numerous psychological stresses. They are increasingly victims of rape, domestic violence, and abuse inside and outside their homes. They are the primary caretakers of their children, and too often they also serve as the caretakers of their elderly parents and of their husband's parents. Moreover, many mothers with young children also work outside the home. Although these pressures may apply to women in many other countries, Israeli women have certain unique problems that derive from the prolonged conflict with the country's Arab neighbors and the constant threat of war and terrorism. Israeli women bear responsibility for guarding the home and taking care of the family when their men are called to reserve duty, which often exceeds 30 days a year. This is a heavy burden and all the more so for women with young children, dead-end jobs, and other responsibilities. It is made even heavier by the fact that the school day in preschools and elementary schools generally ends around noon. It is no wonder that women suffer much more than men from chronic depression.

The founders of the center claim that despite these stresses on many Israeli women, Israel lags behind some other modern societies in its orientation to female health in general and to female mental health in particular. They point out that it is only recently that some Israeli psychologists and other human services professionals have begun to recognize what has been realized outside of Israel for some time—that women are a neglected group in both psychological theory and practice. Little attention has been given to the now widely accepted understanding in Western countries that the norms defining "health/behavior" have been guided by theories developed primarily by men about men. Thus, prevailing health care models in Israel often unwittingly reinforce stereotypic female behavior and traditional role expectations. They tend to focus on helping women fulfill their roles as wives and mothers rather than on providing them with the tools to take charge of their lives.

Three basic convictions motivated the center's founders:

1. Israel's mental health services and therapeutic modalities and interventions are incongruent with the specific psychological needs of women and do not provide adequate responses to their psychological and social problems.

2. Alternative modalities of therapy capable of responding to women's specific needs can be devised and developed only within a new and independent organizational setting.

3. This new setting must be managed and directed by women committed to feminist values and perspectives. Only such a setting can enable and encourage feminist practitioners to give free and concrete expression to their theoretical and practical beliefs.

The establishment of the center was motivated both by the awareness of the specific psychological problems and needs of Israeli women, as perceived from a feminist perspective, and by the personal and professional needs of the founders, who sought an organizational framework that would enable them to develop as feminist practitioners.

Goals and Activities

The motives for the establishment of the center have shaped its primary mission. From its inception, the center's founders have sought to achieve four interrelated goals:

1. to form a service organization that would be affordable by, and accessible and responsive to, women from all social, economic, and cultural backgrounds, whatever their sexual orientation and stage in life

2. to provide therapeutic services to improve the psychological well-being and quality of life among women, their families, and their partners

3. to expose other helping professionals who serve women to feminist values and conceptions so as to introduce feminist perspectives into the Israeli mental health system

4. to raise public consciousness of the psychological problems of Israeli women.

In short, the idea was to form an organization that would serve two major functions: to provide professional counseling services for women and to introduce changes in the attitudes toward women in professional circles and the general population.

During the first two years after the decision to form the center, the founding members were engaged in developing its conceptual basis and formulating its practice beliefs. All the members took an active part in meetings, workshops, and marathons that focused on several key issues: analysis of the psychological and social problems of women in general and in Israel in particular; definition of feminism and clarification of the implications of feminism in clinical work; and exploration of the commitments, responsibilities, and specific tasks of a feminist therapist.

The many long discussions and deliberations enabled the members of the center to get to know one another better on a personal level, created a shared body of theoretical and practical beliefs, and strengthened the members' sense of collectivism and identification with the center's specific mission. Furthermore, the discussions enabled the members to clarify and formulate the main objectives of the center's therapeutic work: to offer women a setting in which they would be encouraged to express and clarify their own needs, both individually and collectively, to give and receive strength from one another, and to use treatment modalities that would increase women's sense of personal power and self-esteem and help them to take charge of their lives and to make positive changes in themselves and in their immediate environment.

The center has two branches—one each in Tel Aviv and Jerusalem, which are Israel's largest urban centers. During its four years of operation, the center has offered the following services:

- individual clinical treatment for women (and in certain cases, also for their spouses)

- group treatment (including groups for women in midlife transition, groups for mothers and daughters, groups for lesbians, and groups exploring sexuality, self-esteem, and friendship)

- assertiveness groups

- orientation groups for new immigrants and for women from distressed neighborhoods

- training of volunteers and workers in other women's organizations (such as the Center for Counseling Rape Victims), with a focus on the special psychological problems of women

- discussion groups for professionals on feminist topics, including the reading and analysis of feminist texts and the examinination of therapeutic interventions from a feminist point of view

- lectures in schools and other settings on women's problems

- special events, such as an exhibition of paintings and photos by survivors of sexual assault, incest, and child abuse; the presentation of movies on the subjects; and a discussion by a panel of experts.

The center's main emphasis has been on the provision of clinical services to women (the first five activities above). It has given little attention to the last three activities, which reflect the center's social change mission: its desire to modify the attitudes of the Israel public toward the psychological problems of women and to introduce change into the Israeli mental health system. The dominance of the direct service function over the social change function stems from two main factors: The high demand from women for the center's clinical services has urged the members to devote most of their time to the service function, and the members themselves have preferred to engage in clinical activities in which they can use their experience and expertise, rather than in social change functions in which their knowledge and skills are limited.

Structure and Dynamics

The idea of establishing a counseling center for women was raised in 1986 by four feminist therapists. They recruited seven other therapists who, like themselves, were committed to feminist values and perspectives. These 11 women constituted the founding nucleus of the "collective" that formed the center, and most of them continue to lead it. Since its formation, three members have left the center for personal reasons and four others have joined it. New members were admitted after a year of candidacy, on the basis of their commitment to feminist conceptions and their professional competence.

The center now has 12 members (three clinical psychologists, two educational counselors with experience in family therapy, and seven social workers with clinical experience). In addition, it employs four nonmember therapists as adjuncts. Because it is currently engaged in formalizing its organization and in broadening its base of external support, it is not recruiting new members.

The unique character of the center as a feminist alternative organization is reflected in its organizational structure and decision-making patterns. From the very beginning, the center's founding members were determined to form a collectively, democratically run organization, with consensual decision making, equal distribution of responsibilities, and total rejection of any hierarchical tendencies. These principles have continued to guide the center ever since. There are regular weekly members' meetings in each of the two branches and monthly meetings of all of the members. These meetings, which are the backbone of the center's democratic structure, serve as the main locus of organizational decision making. There is no hidden organizational agenda. Every matter concerning the center's policies, structure, and professional and administrative activities is brought up and openly discussed at the meetings. The meetings also serve social and learning purposes and contribute to the collective's cohesion.

However, the center is not free of internal controversy, because each of the members brings to the center her own personality, expectations, and needs. Moreover, the members have studied and worked—and most of them continue to work—in a variety of settings and thus have different professional experiences and approaches. This diversity of personalities and professional backgrounds has resulted in conflicting views and perceptions of several organizational and professional issues. The center respects the individuality and independence of its members and therefore allows, and even encourages, open and frank discussion and free expression of opinions and feelings. At the same time, the center makes every effort to reach consensus on controversial issues and to avoid decisions and measures that any of the members opposes. To achieve this end, the members devote a great deal of energy and time, often many hours, to working through controversial issues. Every member is encouraged to express her views, even if she is in a minority, and to try to persuade the others. If agreement is not reached even after long discussions, the tendency is to postpone the decision and to raise the issue again at a later date. In certain cases, the members have opted not to make any decision at all when it might have seriously upset or alienated even one of the members. The members' long and intimate acquaintance, their mutual respect and trust, and their commitment to the collective have all helped to moderate tensions and to foster the strong tendency toward consensus.

Most of the center's administrative chores are performed by the members themselves. An effort is made to ensure that the time spent on maintaining and operating the organization is equally divided among the members. However, if, for family or other reasons, some members have more free time than others, those members will spend more time at the center. Each member undertakes the jobs and responsibilities that suit her competencies, skills, and experience, as well as her wishes and expectations. These tasks include internal administrative work, correspondence and negotiations with other organizations, preparing and chairing meetings, giving lectures, writing reports, supervision, and the like. No member is asked to perform duties that she dislikes. Certain administrative tasks, such as public relations and writing grant proposals, that require special skills not possessed by the members have been transferred to external specialists. About a year ago, the center recruited a permanent administrative secretary who performs some of the tasks previously performed by the members, but the members still spend many hours on administrative work.

As required by law, the center has a board of directors. The board consists of seven women who identify with the center's feminist values and support its mission. However, this board is very passive, and it does not show any interest in influencing the center's policies or intervening in its ongoing activities. Furthermore, the board's contacts with the collective members are very limited; its only activity is to approve once a year the center's annual budget and financial report.

About a year ago, after long consideration, the members of the collective decided to form a board of directors that would play a more active role, especially in mobilizing financial resources and strengthening the center's links with other bodies. The decision to change the board from a passive to an active body was taken to improve the center's financial situation and to broaden its public support. The decision reflects the members' growing concern about the center's financial impecuniosity and its inability to expand the scope of activities so as to make a stronger impact on the community. However, the collective's members are still considering several basic questions pertaining to the structure and functioning of the board: What should its size, composition, formal authority, and concrete functions be? How will new members be selected? What should be the relationship between the board and the collective? Who will make the key decisions and determine the center's activities? These questions have not yet been resolved.

The center's emphasis on democratic management has not been extended to the women who receive its services; the idea of client participation has not as yet been realized in this setting. This may stem from the fact that the center does not have a permanent population of clients from which it can draw an active cadre of participants, as well as from the lack of client demand for participation.

The internal discussions concerning the character of the board reflect a major dilemma faced by the center's members at this stage of its development: how to maintain its unique features as an alternative feminist organization and at the same time successfully deal with the organizational consequences, some of them unanticipated, of these features—notably, the center's uncertain financial basis, its long and sometimes complicated and fruitless decision-making processes, and the heavy administrative burden imposed on its members. The members currently are searching for ways of resolving this quandary.

Interorganizational Relationships

The character of the center as an alternative feminist organization has limited the range of organizations and groups with whom it has established permanent links. The bulk of its links are within the narrow circle of women's organizations that share its feminist perspectives and conceptions. These organizations generally have a few committed activists in leadership positions and a small group of followers. Each of the organizations has carved out a specific niche for itself, and together they cover a wide range of activities in the area of women's issues and problems. The center has established itself as the main organization specializing in women's psychological problems. The feminist movement and a range of women's organizations focus on other targets, such as raising women's political consciousness and political activity, running shelters for battered women and their children, providing professional counseling and emotional support for rape victims, enhancing women's feminist consciousness, and fostering a feminist culture. Yet, despite the feminist common denominator of these organizations, their activists' acquaintance with one another, and their division of labor, the feminist organizations have only limited formal interrelationships. In fact, there are no formal arrangements or bodies that coordinate their activities. This may be so for two reasons: The members of these organizations believe that because many of them know one another, stable coordinating bodies are unnecessary, and the activist's wish to safeguard their organizations' autonomy and independence.

The concrete relationships between the center and other feminist women's organizations go two ways: The feminist organizations refer women who need therapeutic services to the center, and the center counsels these organizations on women's psychological problems and helps them train their staff. The center's relationships with so-called conventional women's organizations are varied in nature and scope. The Jerusalem branch has established strong and permanent relationships with WIZO-Jerusalem. This women's organization has allowed the center to use one of its facilities rent-free for its Jerusalem branch in exchange for free counseling, training, and lectures to its employees and volunteers. This relationship has not been duplicated in Tel Aviv.

Toward the end of 1992, the center obtained limited financial support from another organization, the Women's Forum, that places strong emphasis on women's rights. Additional financial support came from an American organization, Women to Women. Beyond its connections within the circle of women's organizations, the center is making ongoing efforts to mobilize financial resources from other organizations. Over the years, it has applied for assistance to several private foundations and organizations, inside and outside Israel, that support programs designed to improve the social, political, and economic situation of women. Some of the other organizations, such as the New Israel Fund, have provided monies for specific programs initiated by the center. These programs included group work with women from distressed neighborhoods, orientation for women immigrants from Russia and other countries of the former Soviet Union, and the training of professionals working with victims of sexual assault and incest. At the beginning of 1993, financial assistance obtained from the New Israel Fund and the Women's Forum also helped the center to organize a unique event that attracted a great deal of public attention: an exhibition of paintings and photos by victims of sexual assault and incest. The exhibition was entitled "No More Silence—Victims of Sexual Assault and Incest Express Themselves through Their Art."

Until recently, the center refrained from applying for financial support to established public organizations such as government ministries and local municipalities. This approach reflected its wish and need to preserve its independence and to avoid relationships with organizations that might encroach on its autonomy. Not long ago, however, the center deviated somewhat from this principle when it requested a Jewish Agency Foundation grant for one of its projects. (The Jewish Agency is an establishment organization that represents world Jewry in Israel.) The application was rejected. The decision to apply to the Jewish Agency was based on the assumption that this organization would not intervene in the concrete implementation of the project and, consequently, that the center's autonomy would not be jeopardized. The Jewish Agency did not explain its negative decision. The center's efforts to extend its connections with other organizations, including conventional ones, reflects its desire to expand the range of its activities and to improve its financial situation.

However, the center's links with other organizations do not extend to mental health and social welfare organizations, such as community mental health centers and local welfare departments, or to the Ministry of Labor and Social Affairs. The center also refrains from political activity and lobbying for women's issues and has not established ties with political bodies, such as political parties and parliamentary committees.

Thus, the center's limited association with other organizations strongly reflects its full devotion to its service function. The center's refusal to establish ties with formal organizations and political bodies may help it maintain its autonomy as an alternative feminist organization, but it also impairs its ability to achieve one of its original missions—introducing changes into the Israeli mental health system.

Financial Situation

The discussion of the center's interorganizational relationships exposes some aspects of its financial situation. This issue is more fully discussed in this section.

The center's revenues come from three main sources: clients' fees, grants from foundations, and private donations by the center's members. The center's revenues in 1991 were 174,000 shekels (about $62,000). The bulk came from clients' fees for the center's services, especially individual and group therapy services, which range from shekels 60 to shekels 100 (about $20 to $35) an hour. However, because the center is dedicated to serving every woman who needs assistance, even women who can pay only part of the fee obtain help. This policy naturally reduces the revenues the center can collect from this source. Moreover, the center's fees are much lower than those charged by private clinics and, in some cases, by clinics affiliated with the public sector.

In recent years, the center has succeeded in obtaining several small grants from foundations, ranging from $200 to $3,000. These grants generally were used for special center programs, such as the orientation groups for new immigrants and the forementioned exhibition of paintings and photos by victims of sexual assaults.

The funds obtained from the third source, donations by the collective's members, have enabled the center to rent its office in Tel

Aviv and to begin providing services to women there, as well as to fund various administrative and other costs and to cover budget deficits. The center's expenditures in 1991 were about 166,000 shekels (about $59,000). Most of this amount went to salaries paid to the collective's members for their work in the center. All salaries are the same—a member gets 40 shekels (about $14) per therapy hour and 10 shekels (about $3.50) per hour devoted to administrative work or attending meetings. These salaries are considerably lower than those paid in private clinics. A monthly salary is also paid to the administrative secretary, and ad hoc payments (based on work done) are made to the center's accountant and lawyer. Other expenses include the cost of special center programs and maintenance of the center's offices in Tel Aviv (rent, office equipment, telephone bills, postage, and so on) and in Jerusalem, where the center does not pay rent but has the other maintenance costs.

The dependence on low client fees, modest grants from a small circle of organizations, and private donations from its own membership limits the center's revenues. Broader links with other organizations could augment its ability to obtain funds but, as previously indicated, the center has decided to refrain from applying for financial assistance to organizations that could threaten its autonomy. Its uncertain financial basis is one of the major problems facing the center at this stage of its development. The major problems and their implications for the center's continuous functioning as an autonomous alternative feminist organization are discussed next.

Future Prospects

One of the center's major problems is its uncertain economic base and, consequently, its perpetual financial insufficiency, which impinges on its ability to achieve its targets and to grow and develop. Its financial constraints, which stem in part from its character as an autonomous alternative organization in an inconvenient environment, have three negative consequences.

1. The salaries paid to the collective's members are lower than those paid in other clinical settings; therefore, the number of hours members can afford to devote to the center is limited.

2. Many of the administrative tasks necessary for maintaining and operating the center are performed by the collective's members themselves at very low remuneration. It was only about a year ago that the center decided to hire an administrative secretary to do some of the work.

3. The center's ability to expand its activities, to develop and launch projects, to make a stronger impact on the community, and to achieve at least part of its social change objectives is limited.

Currently, the center focuses on its service functions and devotes only limited attention to its broader social and political objectives of influencing the Israeli mental health system and of raising public awareness of the psychological problems of Israeli women.

The members are concerned that these consequences of financial constraint may lead to organizational standstill. This concern is intensified by problems arising from the center's internal structure and ideology.

The special qualities of the center as an alternative feminist organization—democratic management; shared decision making; equal distribution of tasks, responsibilities, and rewards; absence of hierarchy; and a sense of collectivism—constitute its essence and the source of its strength and cohesion. However, the members have begun to feel that the price they are paying for belonging to such an organization, including the time spent in long and frequent meetings, the frustrations of complicated and sometimes fruitless decision-making processes, the tedium of administrative chores, and the low pay for their efforts, is too high.

Concerned that the burden of work and the sense of standstill may erode their commitment to the center, the members have decided to look for new ideas to reenergize the center and stimulate development. One idea is to form an active board of directors to help the center obtain more financial support. Another is to reach out and form more ties with organizations outside the feminist sphere. The members have also decided to consult an expert in organizational management to help them deal with the center's problems. All of these ideas, however, have implications for the collective's future.

Members are wary that implementation of some of these ideas might change the character of the center and alienate members who are dedicated to its unique mission. The main question is whether the center faces a real threat to its continued existence as an alternative feminist organization. Although problems do affect the center's operation at this stage, they do not appear to jeopardize its continued existence. The mutual respect and close relationships among the members and their commitment to the center's principles and to its feminist mission seem to counterbalance the potential threat. In fact, during its many years of existence, the center has kept its democratic and participative character and has not developed noticeable bureaucratic features, unlike quite a few other alternative organizations. The center is now at a crossroad. It is looking for a course of action that will enable it to move forward, to garner more resources, to extend its activities, to develop new projects, and to make a significant impact on the environment, but not undermine its essential features as an alternative organization.

Our conviction is that the center possesses the structural flexibility and the potential to adopt and implement ideas that will enable it to overcome the main problems it faces. These changes may somewhat weaken certain of its cherished characteristics, including the rejection of links with established organizations, the insistence on consensus, and the involvement of all members in every decision. On the other hand, we believe that the other major qualities of the center as an alternative organization, especially its sense of collectivism, absence of hierarchy, commitment to feminist values, and equality of responsibility and pay, will remain intact.

References

Bargal, D., & Gidron, B. (1983). *Self-help and mutual-aid groups in Jerusalem: An exploratory study.* Jerusalem: Hebrew University, Paul Baerwald School of Social Work.

Eisenstadt, S. N. (1967). *Israeli society.* New York: Basic Books.

Eisenstadt, S. N. (1985). The Israeli political system and the transformation of Israeli society. In E. Krausz (Ed.), *Politics and society in Israel: Studies of Israeli society* (Vol. 3, pp. 415–427). New Brunswick, NJ: Transaction Books.

Friedman, A., Izraeli, D. N., & Shrift, R. (1982). *The double bind, women in Israel.* Tel Aviv: Hakibutz Hameuchad Publishing House.

Katan, J. (1989). Informal social networks and their place in the social welfare arena. *Social Security, 34,* 35–48.

Katan, J. (1990). Welfare services in Israel. In D. Elliott, N. S. Maydas, & T. D. Watts (Eds.), *The world of welfare* (pp. 153–169). Springfield, IL: Charles C Thomas.

Lev-Ari, R. (1992). *After the beating—Women's coping with domestic violence.* Tel Aviv: Naamat.

Neipris, J. (1978). *Social welfare and social services in Israel: Policies, programs, and issues in the late seventies.* Jerusalem: Hebrew University, Paul Baerwald School of Social Work.

Shmueli, A., Shoval, J., & Fleishman, R. (1983). The informal support for the elderly, social networks in Bakaa neighborhood in Jerusalem. *Social Security, 25,* 68–78.

CHAPTER SEVEN

New Zealand
The Society for Research on Women

Miriam Vosburgh and William W. Vosburgh

The small island nation of New Zealand is located in the South Pacific some 1,200 miles east of Australia, its nearest large neighbor. Although 12.5 percent of its 3.4 million people are New Zealand Maori (Polynesian) and 3 percent are Pacific Island Polynesian, most inhabitants are of European origin and overwhelmingly from the British Isles. The country became part of the British Empire by treaty in 1840 and is still a member of the British Commonwealth. With the living standards of an industrialized society and an economy based largely on the primary industry of exporting wool, timber, and a variety of fruits, the country depends on overseas markets and is highly vulnerable to fluctuations in terms of trade.

From the early beginnings of the British settlement, the New Zealand people turned to government for economic and social legislation to promote and ensure economic security. Alternatives to government were largely lacking in an extremely isolated country with no wealthy elite and no large-scale domestic industry. Pressures on the state to assume wide-ranging responsibilities tended to increase over time and reached a particularly high level during the economic depression of the 1930s. The country's first Labour Government responded with the Social Security Act of 1938, which introduced a comprehensive set of social programs with a mixture of universal and means-tested benefits and a series of economic measures designed to safeguard the economy by bringing it closely under government control. The legislation included a universal health care system. These measures heralded a period of increasing central control and the development of an archetypal "welfare state," which survived for nearly half a century. Since that time, revolutionary political, economic, and social changes have occurred. Two stages in this process may be distinguished, the first from 1974 to 1984 and the second from

1984 to the present. The Society for Research on Women in New Zealand, Inc., the subject of this chapter, was founded in 1966 and remained active for 25 years. It experienced all phases and was profoundly affected by the eclipse of the welfare state.

Throughout the 1960s, a National Party Government was in power. Despite being the more conservative of the two major parties in New Zealand, it maintained moderate socialist policies, such as keeping stringent regulations on the economy, government ownership of major means of production, and the structure of social provision including national health and education systems. At that time, there was still an expansive approach toward the provision of social services, embodying long-standing community values of mutual care.

The period from 1974 to 1984 encompassed sustained governmental attempts to maintain the economic and social status quo in the face of mounting economic difficulties, including an oil crisis in 1973 and 1974, a sharp drop in trade at that time. Later in the decade, New Zealand experienced a second oil crisis and the loss of its preferential markets in Great Britain when the latter joined the European Economic Community. Government attempted to shore up the economy and maintain existing social provision through extensive overseas borrowing, increasing subsidies to domestic industries, tighter government economic regulation, and grandiose industrial development projects. These strategies did not work.

In 1984, reacting to the perilous state of the economy, the voters swept a Labour Government into power, hoping it would pull the country out of its difficulties, as a previous Labour Government had done in the depression of the 1930s. The new government took completely unexpected approaches. Informed by monetarist economics, minimalist ideas of the role of the state, and skepticism about the extent of government responsibility for the individual, the new government brought about devolution and divestiture of state activities and reliance on business-like organizational forms and market mechanisms. The substance of these changes has included severe challenges to "centralism" and state planning, as well as acceptance of a fairly high level of the social costs (such as unemployment) of radically changed economic policies touted as necessary and inevitable (James, 1986; Johnston & Von Tunzelmann, 1987). Although such major social provisions as the health and education systems were reorganized under the Labour Government toward more private provision and community involvement, change in the welfare system came only after the election of a National Party Government in 1990. At that time, the rapid growth of welfare dependency rates, partly resulting from an increasing rate of unemployment, led to cuts in welfare benefits and a greater amount of means testing to determine eligibility (Shannon, 1991).

On an international level, the New Zealand experience over the past half century has not been unique. As many Western societies introduced socialistic measures in the 1930s, welfare states subsequently expanded, and social and economic philosophies and conditions changed, there has been a large-scale withdrawal of state involvement in many areas of life. In New Zealand, however, the swings have been unusually rapid and radical. Until the early 1980s, a large part of the New Zealand economy was run by the state, and its social provisions were comprehensive and often innovative. In the past decade, however, private property, competition, market forces, individual contracts, and welfare retrenchment have prevailed.

Women's Movements and the Emerging Problems of Women's Rights

Ideologies and laws brought to New Zealand by British immigrants in the 19th century included, on the one hand, the democratic ideals that were inspiring women's struggles for equality in the British Isles and, on the other hand, laws dictating male-only franchise and other preferential rights for men. Consequently, agitation for women's suffrage, as well as rights to higher education, admission to the professions, and rights over property and offspring, began very early in the country's history. New Zealand women had greater status than British women in general, arising in part from their importance as workers in a recently settled, agricultural country. Their status helped to strengthen their demands. It was an organized women's movement, informed by a worldwide ideology and composed of a number of organizations—including New Zealand's highly influential Women's Christian Temperance Union—that engaged in separate and unified campaigns and saw many of its demands satisfied by Parliament in the 1890s. The vote was granted to women in 1893, making New Zealand the first country in the world to legislate women's suffrage on a national basis (Grimshaw, 1972).

Success in meeting its major goals led to the demise of the first women's movement, as was the case internationally, but the task of achieving equal rights for women had not been completed. Many women's organizations continued to work individually for social and women's rights (Sutch, 1973). It was not until some years after World War II, however, that signs of the emergence of a second feminist social movement began to appear. Social and economic changes necessitated by the war, among them the increased role of women in the work force, clearly exposed the inequalities between men and women in occupational conditions, pay, and domestic responsibilities. Women's organizations played a major part in attempts to correct this situation. Protest actions and lobbying the government for policy changes, often in combination with professional groups, trade unions, or other organizations, were frequently used strategies. In more than one case, women's groups actually joined with government to achieve change. This approach was possible because the government at the time was relatively favorably disposed toward providing greater community protection for individual citizens, including women.

The first success of note was the achievement of "equal pay for equal work" in the public services, covering some 20 percent of both male and female workers in New Zealand. Long-term efforts to secure equal pay for this significant section of workers had culminated in the late 1950s with the formation of an Equal Pay Council that included all major women's organizations, as well as a variety of other groups. The council strongly supported the demands of the Public Services Association (the public services workers' industrial union) for the abolition of gender discrimination in pay and work conditions. The government responded by passing the Government Service Equal Pay Act in 1960. Proponents of women's rights hoped that the unions of private sector industries would follow the Public Services Association by adopting equal pay principles and insist that these principles be implemented in the wage contracts that unions negotiated periodically for each industry. Progress in extending equal pay to the private sector was, however, slow.

In 1964 a Joint Committee on Women and Employment, representing the major women's organizations, was founded to lobby government to take further action in the women's employment area. Committee efforts led to the establishment in 1967 of a National Council on the Employment of Women (NACEW), whose charge was to advise the Parliamentary Minister of Labour of needed changes in women's employment opportunities and conditions. NACEW is a joint citizen and government venture with members that include the major national women's organizations and management and labor, as well as government appointees and representatives.

The Society for Research on Women in New Zealand, Inc., (SROW) also was founded in this environmentally favorable period. It was, however, a voluntary group, indeed an alternative organization—founded by women to provide social planning information about women and their lives (Perlmutter, 1988). The more radical components of the modern women's movement, namely the Women's Liberation Front, had become an organized force by the beginning of the 1970s. This part of the movement adopted a large range of feminist goals from moderate to extreme and emphasized the feminist method, including democratic participation in groups, no fixed roles, and consciousness-raising as the preferred technique for motivating protest and changing women's lives (Dann, 1985).

The women's movement contributed toward and also reflected the increasing participation of women in the public sphere. For example, between the censuses of 1966 and 1986, the percentage of women of working age—ages 15 to 64 years—and in paid employment rose from 35 percent to 63 percent. In the later decade, a particularly large part of the increase was constituted by women aged 25 to 34 years. This can be explained partly by the rising average age of women at the birth of a first child and partly by a steady rise in the proportion of mothers undertaking employment while their children were still young. Over the decade, the proportion of working mothers with a child under one year of age rose from 12 percent to 21 percent; with a child age one to four years, from 22 percent to 34 percent; and with a child age five to nine years, from 38 percent to 51 percent. At all ages, women with a university education were more likely than others to be in the full-time labor force (Haines, 1989).

Network interactions and overlap among the disparate components of the women's movement were dense, encompassing both private and public associations. Many goals were held in common. Although emphases and degrees of specialization differed, all groups were committed to the achievement of social, political, and economic equality between men and women, and many groups stressed the goal of autonomy for women in all major life choices. There is still a distance to go before these goals are fully achieved.

The Underlying Values

In the mid-1960s, when SROW was founded, the welfare state and the ideas and values that it represented were central to the way New Zealand thought of itself as a nation. At that time, the welfare state would surface early in any conversation concerning what was distinctive about the country as a whole. New Zealand had retained close cultural and economic identification with Great Britain to a much greater degree than neighboring Australia, where the urge for independence in thought and deed compounded by Britain's apparent readiness to abandon Australia to the Japanese in 1942 had led to increasing ambiguity. Britain emerged from World War II and began building a welfare state in earnest under the aegis of the British Labour Party, and New Zealand was happy to discover that it had anticipated many of these welfare state developments. New Zealand had developed its welfare state in a more or less pragmatic fashion but found the ideology developed by Fabian thinkers and philosophers such as Richard Titmuss especially sympathetic.

The values bound up in the welfare state included broad action by government to deal with social conditions and problems; centralized planning in the social and economic spheres; commitment to a rational planning model in which problems were framed, alternatives examined, and choices in public policy made by reference to detailed information; and a fundamental, underlying egalitarianism that reinforced commitment to industrywide wage agreements and universal benefits. The planners were heavily committed to scientific research to ensure the accuracy of information used in planning. Although they realized that science could not make choices for them, they did believe that sound information would lead ultimately to sound choices.

The New Zealand welfare state reached its apogee in the early 1970s. Since the late 1950s, however, occasional voices of discontent have been raised, often deploring the apparent dullness of society and the tidiness of people's unchallenged lives. These voices summed up their criticism in the mocking reference to the country as "Godzone," a contraction of "God's own country." In spite of this occasional and fairly gentle social criticism, the welfare state and its philosophy represented an expression of secure values.

A deeper, more fundamental value had been with the New Zealand society almost since its inception in the last century. This value was a spirit of community that took the form of mutual obligation and mutual aid. New Zealand was a place where people helped one another, and there was a continual preoccupation with ensuring that if people got ahead it was not at the expense of others and that everybody was ensured the basic necessities of life. This, of course, was coherent with the welfare state and reinforced its development.

When it arose in the 1960s and 1970s, the most recent New Zealand women's movement began with attention to the problems that had been articulated by women elsewhere in the world and to the central question of just how New Zealand stood in its treatment of women. On the one hand, the international women's movement and some occasional local voices decried things that very probably were wrong. On the other hand, the national pride in being a progressive society (after all, women had obtained the vote as early as 1893) presented the hope that things might not be that much out of order. It is interesting to note in this connection that the country firmly believed that in the 1950s and 1960s it had solved any problem of relations with its racial minorities and that the country was a living example for places with more turbulent racial histories—an illusion that was decisively shattered in the 1970s.

If militant action in a style that was emerging throughout the world and that was to become the hallmark of the 1960s and 1970s provided the wrecking ball with which to batter unsatisfactory structures, where were the building blocks for new and more just ones to be found? What were the problems that had to be examined? What exactly was the condition of women? What would constitute an agenda for orderly, permanent change? The answers to such questions were not to be found readily. SROW moved into this vacuum and, in addressing the need for information, created a niche for itself in the movement and for many years in the larger society as well.

The structure and functioning of the welfare state, with its commitment to the state as the agent for solving social problems or meeting changing conditions and its commitment to the rational planning model and to scientific social research, were more or less assumed by SROW as the environment in which it was to do its work. In addition, the national ideal of people helping one another was specified to women helping women. SROW thus had a firm anchor in secure values, which was to be a source of strength until the mid-1980s and the sudden arrival of the "revolution."

The precarious values (Clark, 1956) that informed SROW were ones that it shared with the women's movement in general. Both groups favored removal of all barriers to women's full participation in society and the reordering of society's reward system. They were antibureaucratic, suspicious of professionalism as a source of authority, devoted to egalitarianism and consensual decision making, and regarded small face-to-face groups as the significant organizational units. Although some of these commitments may not appear radical, they all arose from a dissatisfaction with, and critique of, structure and process in the wider society.

SROW: The Beginnings and the Mission

The resurgence of feminism in New Zealand in the 1960s was linked to a movement found throughout the industrialized world. Writings on women, from academic discussions of their changing role and its implications to more radical analyses of their oppression, were read and discussed by large numbers of New Zealand women. Examples of many problems outlined in the literature could be clearly seen in New Zealand society—inequalities that always had existed or that had been created or exacerbated by more recent social and economic change. Two facts became increasingly salient to the women who founded SROW:

1. Government policies concerning women's employment and family lives required further change to fit the new philosophies and new situations. New consciousness and new analyses of the position of women called for further action, even in such a progressive situation as New Zealand's.

2. Information on women and their lives, required as a basis for planning these social and economic changes, was almost completely lacking.

Neither governmental research units nor social sciences departments in universities nor any other research agencies had produced the necessary data, and they were not planning to do so. This task was to be the mission of SROW.

The founding of SROW in 1966 was triggered by a chain of events beginning with a broadcast of the Voice of America Forum lectures, "The Potential of Women." Motivated by the broadcast, a group of women in Wellington, New Zealand's capital city, set up a lecture series to examine similar issues in a local context. The immense interest generated by the lectures led to the formation of SROW (Shields, 1971).

SROW (1966) expressed its main objectives as follows:

- to examine from time to time the attitudes of individuals, groups, and the community toward the education of girls and their subsequent employment; the factual situation; and the needs of girls and women

- to publicize the findings in the appropriate quarters

- to endeavor by all appropriate means to bring about desirable change

- to further in every way possible the general interests of women in New Zealand.

Thus, the central objectives of the organization were the building up and dissemination of a credible, reliable, and extensive body of information on the condition of women. Its functions were not, however, to be restricted to research and publication but were to include other "appropriate" activities furthering the interests of women. Beginning early in its history, SROW became an advocate for women's rights and opportunities under certain conditions that will be discussed in a later section.

In summary, the conditions that shaped SROW from its earliest days were as follows:

- With the launching of the women's movement, an absence of reliable information created difficulty in raising consciousness, articulating needs, and seeking solutions. Not only was this a clear societal failure but, because of traditional modes of organization and scarcity of resources, it was a situation that was likely to continue.

- Trends in education and family structure had led to the presence of a pool of educated women anxious to use their talents and training. Because many of these women had domestic responsibilities, flexibility was a prime consideration. The attraction for such persons to social research was great. However, these circumstances narrowed the organization's social base somewhat.

- The traditions of New Zealand society, which has regarded government as generally benevolent and as a vehicle for addressing social problems, had been heavily reinforced starting in the 1930s with the emergence of the welfare state and subsequent social engineering. The welfare state also had been heavily committed to the rational planning model, which required a large body of accurate information for legislation and program design. These circumstances created an atmosphere in which gathering information was a normal and natural procedure. Furthermore, although the information needed was that dealing generally with the condition of women, even studies that were highly localized or keyed to specific problems added to the general store of knowledge.

- The emerging ideology of feminism, particularly the idea of women helping women, gave impetus to SROW. Not only would SROW help other women by closing the information gap as time passed, it would also give women a chance to learn and become involved in an activity unusual for many of them at that time. Their own consciousness would be raised while raising that of other women and of the society in general. Feminist ideas about organization also shaped the group's structure and created a major pressure toward evolving an organizational form well suited to the groups' needs.

Structure and Governance

During its first two years, SROW had a simple, centralized structure designed to support one large project at a time. By 1968, however, it had branches in the cities of Auckland, Wellington, Christchurch, and Dunedin, and SROW had to create a new extended structure for the organization. Several imperatives, well recognized by the leadership, guided the change. First, with members ranging from a few with advanced research skills to those with none, it was important to separate administrative groups from research committees to give those members not yet trained in research a useful role. Second, SROW had to ensure continuing research activity at the branch level to sustain enthusiasm and encourage creativity. This need led to the creation of grassroots study groups through which research projects could be devised, organized, and carried out with the support of the branch structure (Shields, 1971). Finally, the need for central supervision of projects to ensure high standards resulted in the establishment of a chain of committees through which research proposals would progress from a branch standing committee to a national projects committee that would provide technical help and support for funding applications, when requested.

The structure at the national level consisted of administrative committees and the all-important projects committee. The national executive of elected officers, which was the chief administrative committee, was located in Wellington. It met once a month and maintained communication with branches through meetings, the research process, a newsletter, and personal friendships. The organization, then, was hierarchical to some extent. This was necessary so that

- the organization could exert sufficient control over the research process and outcomes to ensure that the research met high standards of quality, relevance, and objectivity

- its structure would allow for interactions with outside organizations (especially government) with which SROW needed to relate for resources and recognition (Pennell, 1987, 1990).

In practice, however, the branches had a considerable amount of autonomy, through keeping part of the membership subscription payments, electing their own officers, making their own rules (compatible with national objectives), and originating research projects and carrying them out. The national body set broad research policy, maintained data on ongoing research projects, and arranged for publication and distribution of studies.

As SROW evolved, it took on the overall organizational form of an "adhocracy"—a cluster of changing projects staffed by small work groups with a minimal superstructure to service them and conduct routine business (McHugh & Mintzberg, 1985; Mintzberg 1979; Waterman, 1990). This evolution appears to have been generated by the dominance of the small discussion groups and the projects they undertook as the basic organizational units. This organizational form is found in research and development organizations that undertake a number of projects, often unrelated (Smith, 1966). In the case of SROW, it was reinforced by localism. At the same time, feminist ideas about organization kept the central structure minimal and offset pressures toward bureaucratization and professionalization. The result, crescive and not deliberately imposed, was a structural form that met the needs of SROW admirably and was fully coherent with feminist organizational principles as they emerged and were codified in the 1970s and 1980s (Ferguson, 1984; Pennell, 1987, 1990).

SROW's operations and system of governance evolved in the light of these values. As they became explicit and codified within the women's movement, one tacit purpose of SROW and other organizations based on these principles was to demonstrate that it was possible to build stable, effective organizations of this type. The returns on a number of counterculture organizations were decidedly mixed (Rothschild-Whitt, 1979). These organizations tended to suffer from displacement of goals to emphasis on means—to worrying almost exclusively about how things were done rather than what or why. Organizations, for example, got so mired in consensual decision making that they had difficulty maintaining any sort of production schedule. SROW, however, escaped major difficulties of this sort, possibly because its structure grew naturally over a long period, providing opportunity for exploring this method of governance.

Leaders, Members, and Organizational Lifespan: Integrity and Survival

SROW's goal to provide planning information for the new policies necessitated by the changing role of women went a great distance toward determining leadership and membership characteristics. Both leaders and members were educated women, many of whom were to undertake further education. Most also were married with children and, in the early years of SROW, were not employed outside the home (Shields, 1971).

The leadership was unusually stable. The presidents and members of the executive committee almost always served the maximum term permitted and often took on other leadership posts when a particular term ended. Long periods in office were caused partly by the difficulty of recruiting new leaders with appropriate qualifications. In turn, the stability of the leadership tied SROW closely to its original objectives.

Participation in SROW's research was welcomed as a socially and intellectually satisfying activity during the housebound phase of members' lives. Over time, however, "the membership changed from being mainly women at home with young children to those in paid employment, many in the research field" (Mowbray, 1982, p. 2). This development reflects the changing pattern of women's employment in New Zealand described earlier and served to reduce the pool of young well-educated mothers with time to undertake voluntary research—a factor in SROW's declining membership.

Voluntary organizations of this type have difficulty in sustaining a constant membership. In addition to the more fluid nature of membership in voluntary as opposed to contract organizations, in general, research tasks are sometimes demanding, labor intensive, and tedious. The response of some members was to withdraw, putting more stress on others, thus stimulating dissatisfaction and further membership loss. Trends in membership size, therefore, were partly a reflection of the nature of SROW's activities.

The formation of SROW was accompanied by a rapid buildup of membership to more than 1,100 by 1968. Since then there have been fluctuations, but overall numbers decreased to the 200s by 1987. The formation of new branches and successful recruitment efforts occurred when the initiation of new projects demanded larger numbers of workers for tasks such as interviewing and coding. Membership declines resulted from the opposite conditions—the closing of branches and the completion of research projects. These factors were internal to SROW. External reasons for the membership declines stemmed from a number of societal changes:

- The change in the employment patterns of young mothers influenced membership size very directly by eliminating for many the housebound stage during which they found the part-time, intellectually and socially satisfying activities offered by SROW to be an attractive option. It is possible, indeed, that the efforts of SROW to facilitate maternal employment have been partially responsible for reducing its membership base. Furthermore, the research training SROW has given to its members has equipped a number of them to enter the work force, sometimes in a research capacity. Leadership experience also has helped national officers in particular to obtain highly skilled jobs and influential positions. Some officers have been appointed to university faculties, for example, and two were elected to Parliament, became cabinet ministers, and, successively, held the portfolio of Women's Affairs.

- The emergence of single-issue organizations, often sponsored by members of the Women's Liberation Front in its later stages and, in some cases, even initiated by SROW members, has led to membership decline in societies with broader substantive interests, such as SROW. Activist associations with a specific focus, such as domestic violence, environmental conditions, and women's health care, have absorbed the time and energy of increasing numbers of women (Bunkle, 1992; Coney, 1988). Many key informants regarded this as the most important reason for the decline.

- It is probable that SROW's objectives now appear less salient to its customary membership base. Research findings on women and their lives, including those of the SROW studies, have accumulated. Furthermore, some research on women's issues now is being undertaken by other bodies, such as the Women's Studies Association and women's studies programs in the major universities. Although there still is much research to be done, many women perceive the need for research as less urgent than was once the case.

- Revolutionary political and economic changes, beginning in 1984 with the election of the Fourth Labour Government and continuing with the return of the National Government to power in 1990, have created a highly turbulent environment over the past nine years.

The dazzlingly rapid changes introduced by the Labour Government produced a high level of confusion and uncertainty. It was impossible to predict how women's issues would be affected overall. Clearly, the government gave these issues some lip service and created the Ministry of Women's Affairs in 1984 to assist in improving the status of women, but little substantive change beneficial to women seems to have occurred. It was also this government that eliminated SROW's annual research grant.

The National Government has since made changes unfavorable to women in several social programs—for example, the Accident Compensation program in which benefits to nonearners, the bulk of whom are women, have been greatly reduced (Gaskins, Kronick, & Vosburgh, 1979). The government's major effect on an organization like SROW, however, comes from changing the role of government and other value premises of the welfare state. For example, changes mandating individual negotiation and reliance on market mechanisms in lieu of the customary New Zealand adherence to collective bargaining and conditions of universality in such areas as education, employment, health, and other services have changed the rules of the game for women's pay equity issues. SROW was particularly critical of an Employment Contracts Act passed in 1991, whose effects SROW evaluated as follows: "The Act has altered all the ground rules previously established between employer and employee. Virtually all conditions of employment are now negotiable" (SROW, 1991, p. 26). The act has devalued rational planning, making it impossible, for example, to work toward achieving national laws facilitating the employment of women and conditions such as part-time work, job sharing, or reduced work hours during school vacations. This changed economic approach has undercut the mission of societies like SROW and has discouraged current and potential members.

SROW membership was beginning to decline quite steeply by the end of the 1980s, putting its future in doubt. At the Annual General Meeting of 1991, it was decided to disband the national organization. Two branches, Wellington and Christchurch, elected to continue but are operating without a national structure. Christchurch is pursuing a vital project on the effects of economic depression on families—a project central to SROW's mission—whereas Wellington believes that its mission is not yet completed.

Activities, Advocacy, and Controversy

From 1966 to 1991, SROW published over 70 pieces of work; the majority were research reports and the others a miscellany of manuals, bibliographies, and compendia of lecture series. SROW aimed at wide distribution for the research studies. For the members involved, these studies represented the products of their labor as well as a continuing source of income for the group as a whole. The publications were available commercially and also were deposited in university and public libraries.

Research topics were closely tailored to the title and goals of SROW, reflecting a fair consensus on values and interests. Topic areas were central to the everyday lives of women. The areas could be broadly classified as becoming a parent, parenthood, quality of life for families, education and employment, and gender-related issues.

Social survey was the major method used, and facts, attitudes, and problems in each area were investigated. Attempts also were made to discover the support services and other policy and program changes needed to increase women's opportunities and to improve their lives and those of their families.

The evidence shows that SROW members always considered producing and publicizing relevant, sound research findings to be their major function. SROW's major strategy was indirect action, a concept that is analyzed later in this chapter. Advocacy, however, also was considered important. This almost always took the form of making written or oral submissions to policy-making bodies. There were few years in which SROW did not make one or more submissions to Royal Commissions (convened by the Crown to investigate and make recommendations on national issues), Parliamentary select committees, cabinet ministers (members of the highest council of government), or other policy-making bodies. Submissions, based on SROW's own research findings, were made on child care, maternity leave, early childhood education, family health counseling, equal pay, single parenthood, and many other issues.

Tensions arose when some members wanted to make submissions on issues that SROW had not researched. On one hand, there were members who believed that SROW had a duty to speak out on all issues affecting women. This group based their stance on SROW's goal "to further in every way possible the general interests of women in New Zealand" (SROW, 1966, p. 1). On the other hand, there were members who insisted that SROW's credibility depended on restricting its scope to areas in which it had done research. A case in point was a disagreement over making a submission opposing restrictive change to the 1977 Royal Commission on Contraception, Sterilization, and Abortion. The decision to make the submission led to a sharp controversy and the resignation of several SROW members.

In general, however, SROW, in seeking to preserve its reputation for scientific soundness, remained rather conservative in its approach to advocacy. Consequently, some members who wanted to be more politically active joined other organizations with a more active stance—often, but not always, also retaining their SROW membership.

SROW's information was intended for use in the societal processes of planning and program development; this meant that it could not involve blatant propaganda, prejudiced techniques, or mere passing observation: The information ultimately would have to prove valid and reliable. The way to ensure the necessary credibility lay in strict adherence to the canons of social scientific method—that the information produced should aspire to the standards of government and university research.

It would, of course, strain belief to imagine that a voluntary group of varied backgrounds could suddenly produce research in volume that met professional standards. The commitment to social research did, however, provide a clearly codified and widely shared and understood standard that, to the extent met, would ensure the necessary credibility and potential acceptance of the work. SROW provided a standard to which to aspire.

The commitment to social research influenced SROW in other ways as well. It provided a vehicle for organizing and planning activities. It involved jobs adapted to a wide range of social and technical skills, allowing most members to find a way to use those skills they had or to learn new ones. Because most projects grew out of group discussions, members exchanged knowledge and opinions in the planning process and gained new perspectives in the field, in analysis, and in the discussion of results.

How the organization should be structured was another source of tension, particularly in its earlier history. Even mildly bureaucratic structure is not inherently compatible with the principles of feminist organization that were gaining currency in SROW's earlier years, namely, egalitarianism and consensual decision-making processes, together with an abhorrence of hierarchical structures and the establishment of roles based on expert knowledge (Ferguson, 1984). SROW, an integral part of the women's movement, was very much in tune with the emerging feminist structural principles. Consequently, occasional controversy and conflict among members resulted from the discrepancy between SROW's structure and feminist organizational principles. Over time, however, the organization adopted an adhocratic form that partially solved the problem.

The first members of SROW did not evolve their basic strategy through a formal decision process. The commitment to a strategy of indirect action arose from a combination of general conditions in the society at large, consciousness of an unfulfilled need, and the characteristics of the organization's membership. The members probably did not think of it then, and perhaps do not think of it now, as "indirect" action (Vosburgh & Vosburgh, 1993). This is a term the authors of this chapter used to characterize SROW's social action methods meant to indicate that one of the organization's chief characteristics has been the avoidance of such "direct" actions as marches, sit-ins, boycotts, confrontations, and propaganda, which have explicit targets, are directly linked to developing events, and employ emotive and nonrational means such as martyrdoms, demonstrations, and propaganda. (Passivity does not distinguish direct action: Many nonviolent direct action tactics are essentially passive, including boycotts and bringing information to the attention of a commission rather than hoping it will be discovered.) Indirect action follows another route to raising consciousness: that of providing substance for discussion, policy development, and choice. The members learn about the conditions that affect them and about the possibility of ameliorative action through formal investigation, and they hope both to provide a basis for discussion among themselves and to influence others beyond their bounds. Indirect action is keyed to the political processes of agenda setting, policy formulation, and program design and implementation—to the rational planning processes in society.

Indirect action also dovetails with the basic feminist activity of consciousness raising. The members expand their own knowledge of problems and conditions and are able to pursue facts and local examples to inspire awareness on the part of other women and society in general. They are able to equip themselves and others with a foundation for debate and rational public discussion.

Although indirect action can be seen as complementing direct action in a general social movement such as the women's movement, it is difficult to encompass the two modes in a single organization. SROW's experience highlights this problem nicely—the need to protect credibility ruled out irrational tactics or appeals. Militants, on the other hand, have become suspicious of delaying action to "do a study" or "gather the facts" as stalling tactics on the part of the weakly committed or even of the opposed.

Interorganizational Relationships

The most salient interorganizational link for SROW was that with a review committee established by government to administer the grant it provided toward SROW's research expenses. Following an early decision to seek funding from government, a delegation of SROW members obtained an annual research fund from the Ministers of Labour and Finance considered fairly substantial by New Zealand standards at the time. A Research Fund Administration Committee (RFAC) was established with representatives from several government departments, one from the Victoria University of Wellington, and one from NACEW. The RFAC met twice a year to consider the funding of proposals. It evaluated research design, methods, factual accuracy, feasibility, intended use of results, and cost estimates. There is no evidence that the RFAC attempted to evaluate the choice of research topic or that it had a substantive research agenda of its own or refused to fund a particular project for political or other reasons extrinsic to the merits of the research proposal. Theoretically, the RFAC could have compromised SROW's autonomy by influencing its choices of research topics. There are, however, several reasons, apart from the lack of direct evidence, for concluding that this did not happen. First, the branches could (and sometimes did) find alternative funding sources for a particular project; second, research projects that were nationally sensitive may well have been turned down for funding had political criteria been used in the evaluations, but they were not. For example, one potentially controversial project that studied unmarried mothers was funded for three years to study the particular problems of this group, especially those related to money, housing, and work (SROW, 1975).

The RFAC functioned until 1988 when all government liaison with women's organizations was transferred to the new Ministry of Women's Affairs, established by the Fourth Labour Government elected in 1984. The grant was terminated at that time and efforts to obtain regular funding from other sources were not successful. SROW however, had internal sources of revenue, the most important of which were yearly membership subscription fees and profits from sales of research reports and other publications. Although these monies were not sufficient to fund the immense amount of research undertaken, they helped to satisfy SROW's financial needs and so encouraged ongoing efforts at membership recruitment and retention, as well as the maintenance of a significant level of publication.

In addition to SROW's external review committee, the research niche that SROW had carved for itself in the women's movement was complemented by SROW's central position in the movement's organizational networks. Ties ranged from the informal liaison provided by overlapping memberships to sending delegates to national and international meetings, to formal representation on standing committees of several other women's organizations, to performing services for other organizations, to formal participation with others in joint ventures.

Because of SROW's commitment to indirect action, individual members who wished to use more radical methods joined activist groups as well, often creating liaisons with organizations within the Women's Liberation Movement. It was also common for SROW members to join other organizations with research potential, such as the Women's Studies Association, and to promote and support the research function of these groups.

As a group, SROW has acted in a research advisory capacity to several organizations, including the National Council of Women; the Women's Division of the Federated Farmers; and "Te Rapuora," the Maori Women's

Welfare League. It sponsored the formation of the Women's Electoral Lobby and worked with it to complete a study of school committees and women's part in them (SROW, 1977). In turn, other women's organizations have often assisted SROW. For example, when SROW was short of interviewers for its surveys in smaller areas, bodies such as the National Council of Women and the Women's Electoral Lobby have sometimes been able to supply help.

SROW has had functional links with organizations in the public sector also. Lecture series were often arranged in conjunction with an educational body such as the Wellington Play Centre Association and the Departments of University Extension in both Auckland and Wellington. Although SROW has usually resisted pressures to undertake contract research (Dominy, 1986), it did complete studies for two government organizations—the Women's Advisory Committee of the Vocational Training Council and the Human Rights Commission (SROW, 1981, 1982). Undertaking contract research has been infrequent, however, because of the potential for compromising SROW's objectivity or reputation for objectivity.

Connection with government departments was mainly through the RFAC appointed by government. When the Ministry of Women's Affairs was created in the 1980s, official connections were routed through that body but links were not close or instrumental.

The overall picture of SROW is that of an organization managing to maintain a large measure of autonomy while in active, functional interaction with an extensive range of organizations from many sectors of society. The autonomy did not simply occur but resulted from conscious gatekeeping efforts by leaders who resisted both interactions and the formation of alliances that they believed would compromise SROW's goals (Dominy, 1986).

Summary and Conclusions: Threats from Without, Threats from Within

As dedicated as they are in some measure to precarious values, alternative organizations must continually meet and deal with threats to their existence, their autonomy, and their character (Selznick, 1957). Although threats to their very existence seem to be a category with enormous dramatic potential—conjuring up as it does visions of forcible suppression, involving the law or simply the scorn of a large part of society—many threats are not of this direct nature. Many of them are a matter of compromise to gain resources or internal processes and decisions that play themselves out in ways inimical to the organization's original intent.

SROW, because of its commitment to indirect action, tended not to provoke violent or heavy opposition. Many of its leading members pursued their development by working within the system in institutional areas such as politics or higher education. SROW aims were to provoke change through the established institutional mechanisms, chiefly government. This strategy led it to identify with the rational planning process that had yielded relatively little in gains for women as a group, but that could be mobilized to do so. The need to sustain credibility led to submission to the rigors of scientific social research, again an apparent ratification of established wisdom. The need for credibility also opened the way to possible compromises of SROW's autonomy when external resources were sought. The social base of the organization was relatively narrow and elitist. This facilitated access to some institutional areas but raised questions about the extent to which the organization represented women in general. The need for credibility and the nature of the group of women to whom the group appealed made it look somewhat passive and a bit conservative compared to more militant, confrontational, and flamboyant manifestations of the women's movement. The other edge of the sword is, of course, that these very qualities played a major role in SROW's longevity.

The close ties to the established order and its canons of correct procedure both in gaining and using knowledge would appear to cast a shadow over SROW's autonomy. The most direct environmental impingement came with the acceptance of government funding and the general supervision from RFAC that was one of its conditions. A number of circumstances served to blunt any threat from this quarter, as detailed previously.

From time to time, actions within the organization itself posed the threat of moves toward either bureaucratization or professionalization. A move in either direction would have compromised one or more of the feminist principles of organization that had influenced SROW's development. A move toward professionalization would have rested uneasily with its fundamentally voluntary nature as well, and several such moves were blunted by appeals to voluntarism (Dominy, 1986).

The view of the local branch as the significant organizational unit and of the project as the vehicle for action that was so well accommodated by adhocratic organization caused potential problems. Unless the local branch was especially robust and able to sustain membership at a certain level, activity in a particular local area could cease altogether and prove most difficult to revive. The same flexibility that allowed for expansion and contraction as projects came and went lay at the root of this trouble. Localism also reinforced schismatic tendencies and created tensions among branches. These tensions were epitomized by the final decision to disband on the part of the national organization and by the Wellington and Christchurch branches' decision to continue.

The urge to more militant action arising not unnaturally in a social movement organization occasionally threatened SROW's character. That SROW should be heard on the full range of national issues affecting women, whether or not it had completed the research to fortify such a stand and to advance the discussion, was a tempting prospect from time to time. A return to first principles, however, ruled this out.

Various forces have acted on SROW throughout its life. Submission to any of them would have threatened the organization's character and forced compromise of one or more of the values considered fundamental. In review, these forces were militance versus indirect action; professionalism versus voluntarism; hierarchy in executive projects versus feminist collective values; and finally, environmental turbulence that upset the national commitment to centralized rational planning in favor of privatized competition and market-driven provision.

What Now?

If SROW carries on in any form, as a detached local branch in Christchurch driven by an unfulfilled agenda or as a revived national organization of some sort, it will be faced with a number of problems. Substantial inroads, as noted, have been made into SROW's niche. Its own success, building as it did a substantial body of studies (SROW Publications), has caught up with it in that the need it served has been partially met. The talent pool that it initially tapped has been absorbed to some degree into the labor force, and, although many of the leaders are still active and enthusiastic, their energies are more divided than they once were.

As has been noted, however, the most vexing problems for continuing SROW have been posed by the "revolution." Not only have the welfare state and the rational planning model been put aside by a heavy reliance on "market mechanisms," but privatization has become the order of the day (James, 1986; Jesson, 1987, 1989). The shape of government research will probably move increasingly in the direction of contracting with private sources, particularly for program evaluation. Wellington's skyline already features modern buildings that house local branches of American consulting firms, many of which have been involved in such contracts in the United States. A voluntary association, however talented its members, would have to professionalize very heavily to meet such competition, and SROW has strongly resisted these tendencies in the past.

Among the intangibles of New Zealand life, the obligation of citizens to help one another has always been central. This ideal helped to energize the welfare state, as well as give the idea of women helping women a special force. The changes noted previously, with their emphasis on competition and self-interest and faith in impersonal forces such as the market, have placed this ideal in substantial jeopardy. As Jesson (1989) observed, this small and economically unsophisticated nation has been hijacked by a group of ideologues. As this ideology runs its course, there is absolutely no doubt that things will never be the same again. And there is some doubt as to whether they will be better.

References

Bunkle, P. (1992). Withdrawal of the Copper 7: The regulatory framework and the politics of population control. In P. Davis (Ed.), *For health or profit? Medicine, the pharmaceutical industry and the state in New Zealand* (pp. 98–118). Auckland, New Zealand: Oxford University Press.

Clark, B. R. (1956). Organizational adaptation and precarious values. *American Sociological Review, 21*, 327–336.

Coney, S. (1988). *The unfortunate experiment: The full story behind the inquiry into cervical cancer treatment.* Auckland, New Zealand: Penguin Books.

Dann, C. (1985). *Up from under: Women and liberation in New Zealand, 1970–1985.* Wellington, New Zealand: Allen & Unwin.

Dominy, M. (1986). *Gender conceptions and political strategies in New Zealand women's networks.* Ann Arbor, MI: University Microfilms International.

Ferguson, K. (1984). *The feminist case against bureaucracy.* Philadelphia: Temple University Press.

Gaskins, R., Kronick, J., & Vosburgh, W. (1979, June). Community responsibility for accident victims: Changes in the New Zealand welfare state. *The Social Service Review, 53*(2), 261–274.

Grimshaw, P. (1972). *Women's suffrage in New Zealand.* Auckland, New Zealand: Auckland University Press and Oxford University Press.

Haines, L. (1989). *Work today: Employment trends in 1988.* Wellington, New Zealand: New Zealand Planning Council.

James, C. (1986). *The quiet revolution: Turbulence and transition in contemporary New Zealand.* Wellington, New Zealand: Allen & Unwin/Port Nicholson Press.

Jesson, B. (1987). *Behind the mirror glass.* Auckland, New Zealand and London: Penguin Books.

Jesson. B. (1989). *Fragments of labour.* Auckland, New Zealand: Penguin Books.

Johnston, J., & Von Tunzelmann, A. (Eds.). (1987). *Responding to the revolution: Careers, culture and casualties.* Wellington, New Zealand: Government Printing Office.

McHugh, A., & Mintzberg, H. (1985, June). Strategy formation in an adhocracy. *Administrative Science Quarterly, 160–197.*

Mintzberg, H. (1979). *The structuring of organizations.* Englewood Cliffs, NJ: Prentice Hall.

Mowbray, M. (1982, August). *The Society for Research on Women in New Zealand, Inc.* Paper presented at the First International Conference on Research and Teaching Related to Women. Concordia: University of Montreal.

Pennell, J. (1987). Ideology at a Canadian shelter for battered women: A reconstruction. *Women's Studies International Forum, 10*(2), 113–123.

Pennell, J. (1990). *Democratic hierarchy in feminist organizations.* Unpublished doctoral dissertation, Bryn Mawr College. Ann Arbor, MI: University Microfilms International.

Perlmutter, F. D. (Ed.). (1988). *Alternative social agencies: Administrative strategies.* New York: Haworth Press.

Rothschild-Whitt, J. (1979). Collectivist organization: Alternative to rational bureaucracy models. *American Sociological Review, 44*(4), 509–527.

Selznick, P. (1957). *Leadership in administration.* New York: Harper & Row.

Shannon, P. (1991). *Social policy.* Auckland, New Zealand: Oxford University Press.

Shields, M. (1971). *A case study of a recent voluntary organization.* Wellington, New Zealand: Wellington Branch of SROW.

Smith, B. L. R. (1966). *The Rand Corporation: A case study of a nonprofit advisory corporation.* Cambridge, MA: Harvard University Press.

SROW. (1966). *Rules for the Society for Research on Women in New Zealand, Inc.* Author.

SROW. (1975). *Solo mothers.* Christchurch, New Zealand: Argosy Press Ltd. Branch.

SROW. (1977). *One in five.* Wellington: Author.

SROW. (1981). *Follow-up study of female radio and TV servicing apprentices,* Pt. 1. Auckland Branch for the Women's Advisory Committee of the Vocational Training Council.

SROW. (1982). *Women and access to credit and finance in New Zealand.* A report prepared for the Human Rights Commission by SROW (Wellington).

SROW. (1991). *What has happened? A review of 25 years of research by the Society for Research on Women, Inc.* Wellington, New Zealand: Author.

Sutch, W. B. (1973). *Women with a cause.* Wellington: New Zealand University Press.

Vosburgh, M., & Vosburgh, W. W. (1993, March). *Strategy and character in a New Zealand feminist organization.* Paper presented at the annual meeting of the Eastern Sociological Society, Boston.

Waterman, R. H. (1990). *Adhocracy: The power to change.* New York: W. W. Norton.

CHAPTER EIGHT

Norway
The Women's Shelter Movement

Kristin Morken and Per Selle

The women's shelter movement is typical of an alternative social welfare organization in Norway. The movement has played and indeed still plays an important role in bringing the abuse of women to the public's attention and subsequently in lending legitimacy to the idea that abuse of women is a serious social problem that requires comprehensive government action. The movement has set up shelters and help lines in a number of Norwegian communities and carries out extensive services. It emerged primarily out of the feminist women's movement and is in fact the most important institutional expression of the modern women's movement.

Understanding the women's shelter movement's special relationship to the welfare state is key to understanding the character of both the movement and the welfare state. This relationship demonstrates the most typical aspects of the Norwegian (Scandinavian) welfare state and also illustrates what it means to be an alternative movement in a "state-friendly" society (Kuhnle & Selle 1990, 1992b).

The Norwegian welfare state regards abuse of women as a public problem and attempts to solve or reduce it through an organization that is relatively removed from the welfare state both ideologically and organizationally. This organization, as with most alternative organizations in Scandinavia, turns toward rather than away from the welfare state. This is a very important feature, and it is necessary to understand its significance. Public financing is considered a right and is an indication from the state that one's work is important; consequently, the autonomy of the organization is not an issue.

A central thesis of this chapter is that the development of the women's shelter movement, both in terms of internal structure and relationship to its surroundings, is not primarily a result of government financing but rather is more closely related to the internal processes and conflicts that are inherent in the organization—processes that were put in motion by the decline of the women's movement.

Postwar Norway: Period of the Welfare State

From 1945 until the end of the 1970s, Norway was a country of economic growth, very low unemployment, and improving standards of living for all levels of society. Public sector involvement in most parts of society increased. This was witnessed in comprehensive and generous social legislation and public service production in health and the social services, as well as in such areas as education, housing, the labor market, employment, and redistribution of wealth. Norwegian welfare services can be characterized as universal and based on the individual's rights. They are more generous than those of the British and more redistributive than continental European welfare systems (Kuhnle, 1990). In discussions concerning various social policy models, reference is often made to a separate Scandinavian—and thus also a Norwegian—welfare model, which may be described as a relatively successful mixture of capitalism, parliamentary democracy, and welfare orientation (Kuhnle, 1990).

Athough private, profit-based (market) welfare services are rare in Norway, this is not the case with voluntary organizations. Historically, these organizations were pioneers in establishing aid programs and institutions within the health and social services sector. The growth of the welfare state resulted in a shift of responsibility to the state, although in some areas voluntary organizations still perform important functions. Even though the public sector covers almost all the institutions' operating expenses, this does not mean that these institutions are publicly owned. Fourteen percent of the beds in general medical hospitals are owned by voluntary organizations, as well as 21 percent of the beds in psychiatric institutions and 35 percent of the beds in institutions for mentally handicapped people. In addition, 60 percent of the beds in institutions for alcohol abusers and 32 percent of the beds in child and youth care institutions are owned by voluntary organizations (NOU, 1988). An estimated three-fourths of centers for care of elderly people are run by voluntary organizations, although these centers are largely financed by the government. In the provision of health care and social services outside institutions, where there is much less regulation, it is assumed that voluntary organizations are much more active than the state. However, despite their extensive voluntary production of services, these organizations are, to a larger degree than in most other countries, dependent on public funding and therefore also closely linked to the state administratively (Kuhnle & Selle, 1990, 1992a, 1992b).

Another important feature of the development after 1945 is the increasing significance of the corporate channel. The direct link between interest groups and government meant that sector interests in primary industries, labor, and business gained greater influence over their own areas of interest; the negotiation table became the central arena for solving conflicts. Subsequently, there has emerged a wide range of interest organizations, including those outside the labor market and production sphere, that try to put themselves into a direct negotiating position with the state. This is exemplified by the establishment of organizations representing various groups of people needing help (Selle, 1993).

Despite the traditional disagreement between right and left wing political parties concerning taxation and levels of public expenditure, a relatively high degree of political consensus exists regarding social reforms (Kuhnle, 1983). As a whole, Norway has experienced very little polarization of political parties in the period following World War II; all of the parties have been "good social democrats." Conservative parties point out that the most important social policy reform, the 1966 formation of the Norwegian National Insurance and Social Security Program, was made by a nonsocialist government.

During the last 10 years, Norway has witnessed a period of economic stagnation, increasing unemployment, and increasing politicization of high taxes and growing public expenditure. The question of privatization of public services was brought to the fore, and various views of the welfare state and its institutional manifestations immediately became more visible, as evidenced in a long-lasting political tug-of-war over whether to allow the operation of private, profit-based hospitals.

Even though the conservatives were more often in power during the 1980s, only marginal changes were made in the basic principles of the welfare state. Nevertheless, an important "change of climate" occurred in this period: the size and form of the welfare state were definitely political issues, and neoliberalist thinking gained ground even within the social democratic party.

In Norway, as in many other countries, issues such as the environment, women's rights, and nuclear disarmament were put on the political agenda by various interest groups and political movements in the 1970s. These popular concerns gradually were acknowledged by the established political institutions, and equal rights were awarded status as an area of government intervention. Norway gained an international reputation as a progressive country in the field of women's rights. However, despite liberal abortion legislation, sex quotas, a wave of "female coups" in local elections, more female members in Parliament and government, and instances of interparty cooperation on women's issues, Norway still lags behind in such areas as provision of child care and maternity leave.

In conclusion, the central role of the state as problem solver and welfare producer, as well as the basic principle that the welfare state is based on individual rights, has led to the view that it is the state that is primarily responsible for the identification of new health care and social problems. This view must be kept in mind to understand the particular form taken by the women's shelter movement.

Wife Battering: From a Private to a Public Problem

From a historical point of view, Western culture has had a long tradition of subordinating women to men. A woman has been seen as a man's property; for example, in old Norse law the woman is not a party in the marriage contract, she is the subject matter of the contract. Violence of husbands against their wives in many legal systems has been viewed as a husband's right. Roman law allowed the husband to punish or kill his wife if she committed adultery. With the introduction of Christianity to Norway, women lost the right to a divorce if their husbands beat them in the presence of others.

Although it was the women's movement in the 1970s that brought abuse of women to the public's attention and put the problem on the political agenda, there had been similar attempts 100 years before. At that time, feminists and suffragettes tried to achieve similar goals; however, these efforts were on a very small scale in Norway and were primarily expressed by contemporary women authors. In contrast, the feminist renaissance of the 1970s represented a much more radical view of abuse of women and its causes. Such abuse was seen as a combination of direct and structural violence (Alsaksen, 1979; Freeman 1987).

When violence against women again became visible and was put on the political agenda at the end of the 1970s, there were many who doubted the gravity of the problem. But the subsequent rush to newly established shelters indicated that violence against women was not a thing of the past. In recent years the Norwegian health care services alone have handled approximately 10,000 cases of abuse per year (Skjørten, 1988).

Even more surprising was the fact that data from shelters and independent follow-up reports abolished the myth that abuse of women was basically of a psychopathological or sociostructural nature. Among those who sought out the shelters, there was no overrepresentation of women whose husbands did not behave normally either socially or in their jobs (Moxnes, 1981). Nor was there a preponderance of women from the lower levels of society (Malterud, 1981). The myth of violence as a result of the influence of alcohol also was proved to be highly exaggerated (Nisja, 1982).

There were undoubtedly many professionals in health care, psychiatry, and law enforcement who agreed with the women activists of the

1970s who claimed that there was much more abuse of women than was generally believed. Until that time, episodes of violence had been recorded in police statistics as "domestic disturbance," in hospital statistics as "a fall down the stairs," and in pychologists' journals as "anxiety and depression."

Norwegian studies show that battered women often receive very little understanding when they look to the established social services for help, encountering everything from complete indifference to attempts to find fault with the woman as a means of explaining the violence. Furthermore, the same studies indicate that the penal code is not as strictly applied in cases of domestic violence as in cases involving physical assault elsewhere in society (Alsaksen & Nisja, 1980).

According to the Norwegian Social Services Act of 1964, municipal social services offices in Norway are required to provide both counseling and practical and financial assistance to those in social need or crisis. This is still the law. However, social services offices have been criticized for having limited their assistance to the purely financial and for being unresponsive in cases involving people with multiple problems (Bleiklie, 1980; Øyen, 1975). A battered woman often is in the latter category because she may need financial, legal, personal, and housing assistance. The social welfare offices' waiting lists, regulated opening hours, and registration requirements create a situation requiring decisive and planned action on the woman's part, a situation that is highly unsuitable for a woman in an acute crisis. Gradually it has become clear that traditional welfare institutions cannot meet the needs of battered women.

The Women's Shelter Movement: Volunteer Work in a Social Movement

The Beginnings

The women's shelter movement in Norway began when five women from Oslo participated in a tribunal on violence against women in Brussels in 1976. The women were associated with the women's movement and, on returning home to Norway, they began the process of setting up the first shelter group. Their aims were clear from the start: They were going to bring domestic abuse of women to the public's attention, and they were going to run their own shelter. These women considered domestic violence to be a public problem for which the government was obligated to provide funding.

At the start, applications for financial assistance to both central and local authorities were unsuccessful. Nevertheless, the group was able to open a help line in February 1977, with private funds. After the first year of operation, the group was able to prove the need for measures to help battered women: They had received an average of two genuine calls each night. They were given governmental funding for a trial period of two years.

Such was the birth of a nationwide women's shelter movement, which, in the course of a few years, managed to set up and take responsibility for shelters and help lines throughout the country. At the same time, the members of the movement managed to make the media, the politicians, and the public at large aware of the extent and gravity of the problem. Violence against women was gradually redefined; it changed from a private and supposedly almost nonexistent occurrence to what the public generally considered a serious social problem.

By the end of 1991, there were a total of 53 women's shelters and help lines with approximately 3,000 volunteers. Approximately 2,900 women and 2,000 children stayed at the shelters that year. In the same period, the shelters and help lines received 34,000 genuine calls, about 2,000 of which were from children (Barne-og familiestatistikk: Statistikk-Krisetiltak, 1991).

Welfare Ideology

Women's shelters are an alternative source of help for women who have been raped or subjected to psychological or physical abuse. Almost all of the shelters are run by voluntary interest groups—the women's shelter groups—on a nonprofit basis. The members of the groups work shifts, and one or more daytime employees take care of office work and other miscellaneous chores. Only women are allowed to participate in this work.

Whereas the shelters represent a nonprofessional source of help, they also may be characterized as a form of political action—a means of achieving the fundamental social changes required of a society that is completely without oppression of women. Thus, the shelters have an important function as an arena for consciousness raising, both for those who work at the shelters and for those who seek help there.

As a source of help, the shelters provide temporary housing for women who wish to get out of a relationship in which they are abused. Unlike the government social services offices, there are no regular opening hours, waiting lists, application forms, or registration requirements. A woman is able to get help and counseling in obtaining legal assistance, contacting the proper social services, and making any necessary visits to her residence. She also can bring her children.

Women's shelters consider themselves a supplement to government social services and do not aim to replace them. The shelters view themselves as easily accessible special institutions that serve as a kind of transit station between the informal social network and the formal social services structure. One of the goals has been to recruit women with personal experience of abuse to work at the shelters, although this has not been achieved to the degree that was expected. Emphasis is placed on establishing as equal a relationship as possible between users and staff. This is evident in the use of the term "user" in lieu of "client," the term used in governmental social services. Equally important is that it is the woman herself who defines her situation and possible alternative solutions, something that is regarded as impossible within a system based on an unequal user–staff relationship, which tends to deprive the woman of her independence and passify her.

Organizational Form and Political Ideology

Norwegian women's shelters are an offspring of the women's movement, and it was neofeminists and lesbian feminists who founded the first shelter in Oslo. This is significant because there have been two main groups within the Norwegian women's movement. These two groups have been characterized by their particular strategies for change, and these different strategies have influenced their choice of organizational form (Haukaa, 1982).

The Women's Front (Kvinnefronten) emphasized that a strongly centralized and hierarchical organizational structure would create the unity and strength that were considered instrumental in the achievement of political goals. At the same time, increased consciousness was considered possible only in the battle against the external enemy. Politically, this group was far to the left.

The neofeminists, not being that far to the left, opted for a decentralized organization model and a "flat" organizational structure. This organizational structure would contribute to personal consciousness raising and private politicizing; the organization would be more inward looking. Thus, the neofeminists placed greater emphasis on expressive values— the means were just as important as the end. Important features of the flat organizational model include the division into small groups, the absence of elected leaders, the rotation of functions, and the general assembly as the supreme authority. This organizational model, in other words, represents a rejection of the traditional bureaucratic form of organization with a hierarchy and functional division of labor.

The principle of a flat structure has been an important part of the women's shelter movement's ideological foundation. The resistance to a central organization has been strong because there has been a fear that an oligarchical monster would materialize. In other words, a grouping of all shelter groups under one organizational unit would, according to its opponents, lead to a shift of responsibility, authority, knowledge, and activity from the local to the central level. A central organization quite simply would not be consistent with the democratic model on which the women's shelter movement is founded.

Although the women's shelter movement gained support from the Women's Front and from women with relatively little political awareness, the movement from the very start was primarily influenced by the neofeminist school within the women's movement. Their value system was later reflected in both the daily work and external strategy of the women's shelter movement. However, as discussed later, a considerable difference between theory and practice has developed at many shelters. To understand this development, it is important to keep in mind the multiplicity within the movement; it may be regarded as a coalition of different groups of women. To explain changes in the power relationships between these groups, it is necessary to consider external as well as internal factors.

In the autumn of 1980, the Women's Shelter Group (Krisesentergruppa) in Oslo held the first national conference for the country's women's shelter groups. Representatives of 26 groups participated, and the aim of the conference was to promote contact among the groups and to agree on a common platform. From that time on, these annual conferences have been the most important forum for the discussion of goals and strategies for Norwegian women's shelter groups.

At the national conference in 1980, a common platform was passed. It was established that the shelter groups' objectives were to make the public more aware of violence against women and to provide a service for battered women.

Other important resolutions that have been passed at national conferences deal with the recognition of the flat structure as the ideal organizational structure, the principle that there will be compensation for all work done at the shelters, that there will be no external involvement in the organization or operation of the shelters, and that the establishment and operation of the shelters will be funded by the state. To put it briefly, although the women's shelter movement has allocated considerable responsibility for health and social services to the state through financial support, the government will neither govern nor regulate the shelters.

Although national conference resolutions are not binding for the individual shelter, the criterion for full membership in the women's shelter movement is that the individual group adopt the common platform. During the 1980s, there were four groups that remained outside the movement. These groups either were fundamentally opposed to parts of the platform, particularly the principle of compensation for all work, or they did not fulfill the independence requirement because they were run by other organizations.

The women's shelter movement has no central organization but consists of separate organizational units. The debate concerning the establishment of an umbrella organization continued throughout the 1980s, without ever attaining the support of a majority. The possibility of setting up an information office was discussed most recently at the national conference of 1992, but no final decision was made.

Even in Norway, it is rare that a pressure group without a highly formalized structure is given public funds for operations. The fact that the women's shelter movement is publicly funded is indicative of the lucky timing of the movement into the political arena. The movement made its presence felt at a time when the welfare state was at its strongest institutionally and when there was a growing awareness of the weaknesses and limitations of public solutions to social problems.

The women's shelter movement not only exposed abuse, it also proved that battered women had a right to the kind of help that the shelters, in contrast to public social services, could provide. Other groups (for example, the center for incest victims) have followed in the movement's footsteps as a result of the women's shelter movement both establishing a need and representing a qualitatively different service. However, with time, adaptation to both external and internal pressure results in comprehensive organizational and ideological change. These changes are discussed next.

From Movement to Organization

Organizational Model under Pressure

Despite the lack of a central organization, the Oslo group has always served as a natural center for the women's shelter movement. The Oslo group's leading role at the start of the movement established it as the ideological trendsetter and as a source of inspiration and practical advice for the other groups that gradually formed. Furthermore, the Oslo group found itself physically closest to the various national media institutions, governmental departments, and members of Parliament.

The Oslo group also has been the most political of the women's shelter groups. This political orientation was expressed, among other things, in the struggle for compensation for all volunteer work at the shelter. If there was no money left in the budget for wages, the shelter was closed until additional funds were found.

Although the ideal organizational structure in the women's shelter movement is a flat structure, in 1988 there were only three groups organized along these lines. After a "coup" at the Oslo shelter in the autumn of 1989, this number was reduced to two. Therefore, the great majority of the country's shelter groups are of a hierarchical or semihierarchical nature. Even so, most of the groups have incorporated elements of the flat model in their organizations. In 1986 there were only six clearly hierarchical groups (Jonassen, 1987). The remainder have kept the general assembly as the supreme authoritative body. The general assembly may affirm resolutions passed by executive committees or by the executive board itself, either in all matters or those pertaining to internal affairs.

A successful flat organizational structure requires not only a high level of activity but also competence in this form of management. It requires a relatively even distribution of political resources among its members or, if this is lacking, a strong will to work against an uneven distribution. It is not unusual to have an uneven distribution of such resources among women of different backgrounds. Women who have a long history of involvement in women's political organizations or other political activity are better equipped to deal with meeting procedures and better able to articulate their beliefs and to form alliances than are women without such a background. The membership of the women's shelter movement consists of just such a mixed group, and it is likely that in the early years the activists tended to be most influential in making critical decisions.

There is also reason to believe that, in several shelters, such activist domination directly caused the change in organizational form, because the majority felt themselves at the mercy of the more ideologically aware and, therefore, preferred formalized power to informal power structures. Furthermore, the flat type of organizational structure places considerable demands on time and energy, which can be problematic because the practical work at the shelters is also quite resource consuming. This fact, together with a certain degree of external pressure toward a more hierarchical organizational structure, makes it understandable that, at present, the majority of shelters have moved away from the ideal flat type of organizational structure. It remains to be seen whether this is a step in the direction of the more hierarchical organizational structure found in most other voluntary welfare organizations, or whether the shelter groups will manage to maintain elements of their organizational uniqueness.

As mentioned previously, a recurring topic of discussion at shelter movement national conferences is the question of gathering all shelter groups under a national organization. There are several factors that explain why many participants in the movement favor a national organization. First, a national membership would be more heterogeneous in interest and background. Both the movement's start-up phase and its subsequent activity have been characterized by the broad spectrum of types of women and women's organizations involved (Jonassen, 1987). Second, the daily running of the shelters and the constant shortage of funds have taken up most of the groups' time and energy and, as a result, the level of political consciousness has declined, both in general and in the schooling of new members. Many shelters believe they lack the resources to adequately look after their interests and responsibilities outside the shelter itself. This is probably most characteristic of the smaller shelters in less central locations. Additionally, as discussed below, the public funding program consists partly of direct transfers from the central government, and this means that the shelters have a common relationship with the central government.

These features point in the direction of a need for an umbrella organization. It must not be forgotten that most of the shelters have already developed an organizational structure that is of a hierarchical or semihierarchical nature. The step toward a more permanent national organization would not be such a large one for these shelters to take.

Problems of Users and Staff

In theory, shelter users are involved in shelter activities by including long-term residents in the daily work and by recruiting former users to staff positions. However, this has not been as successful as had been expected (Jonassen, 1987). In this respect Oslo stands apart; approximately 30 percent of its staff members at one time were shelter users. Residents also were admitted to the Oslo general assembly, although they seldom attended. It is difficult to determine whether the low level of user involvement is caused by a lack of effort on the part of the shelter group or whether battered women in general do not have the energy to become involved. Nevertheless, studies show that an overwhelming majority of shelter users are satisfied with the help they receive at the shelters, whereas far fewer say the same of government social services (Jonassen, 1989; Skjørten, 1988).

The day staff find themselves in a peculiar in-between position because they often identify with the group members that they are employed to help. They are often their own employer in that they are also ordinary members of the group. These day staff members gain insight into the shelter's daily operation and relation to its surroundings that is completely different from that of the regular members who work one or two shifts per week or month. Members of the day staff are thus in a central position. Research indicates that approximately half of the day staff members influence the decision-making process, either through regular participation in meetings or through their function as secretary of the shelter's executive board (Jonassen, 1987). Generally speaking, the functioning of the shelters is fully dependent on them, and the staff members have probably strengthened their position over time, especially since the contact with local and central government has become more time-consuming and important.

An important consequence of this increased government contact is the fact that, during the 1980s, several shelters were required by their municipal governments to establish an executive committee to be responsible for finances and to have a municipal representative on that committee. Many shelters were opposed to this requirement. However, studies showed that shelters with a formal tie to the municipal government were in better financial condition than those with no such connection (Jonassen, 1987, 1989). In 1988, 16 of 48 shelters had external representatives on their executive boards, and the majority subsequently have expressed satisfaction with this arrangement. In most cases, this involvement is limited to issues of a financial nature, and several external representatives have only observer status on the boards.

Nevertheless, this form of tie to local government is still a controversial issue within the women's shelter movement (Jonassen, 1989). Even the radical Oslo group had to give in at an early stage to the city's demand for representation in the group's finance committee. It was obvious that the public representatives in Oslo found that there was little necessity for supervision; their attendence declined and finally stopped. The women's shelter movement still does not accept shelters with external representatives who have voting rights in all matters pertaining to operation of the shelter.

The women's shelter movement is thus in the midst of change. Most of the groups have ended up with a hierarchical or semihierarchical organizational structure, and it also has become more acceptable to advocate for a national organization. These developments should be considered in light of the primary problem—inadequate funds. In the women's shelter movement in particular, the muffled ideological overtones can be accounted for by the eternal struggle to make ends meet. This is extremely problematic for this type of organization: How does one find the time to reproduce oneself ideologically when service production is the major activity? It is noteworthy that this change is not characteristic of the women's shelter movement alone. The entire women's movement has lost much of its force and ideological essence during the same period.

Women's Shelters: Autonomous, but Public in the Financial Sense

Public Funding Means Legitimacy

With the arrangement of a program for public funding in 1982, the women's shelter movement won the battle for public financing of the shelters. Initially, the program was to be in force for a trial period lasting until 1989. It now seems that funding will continue indefinitely, although the matter has not been officially decided. Because the funds are not provided in accordance with any permanent resolution, the question of continued funding is raised in the consideration of each budget. However, there have not been any signal of change or elimination of the funding. Although this leaves the shelter movement in a somewhat vulnerable and precarious situation, elimination of such funding programs would be very controversial and can almost be ruled out now that reducing or eliminating wife battering has become accepted as a public responsibility.

It should be noted that the public funding program is not explicitly designed for any group within the women's shelter movement. On the contrary, it is open to any voluntary group that is involved in help to battered women. But as previously mentioned, there are actually only a few shelters that are run by voluntary or governmental organizations outside the women's shelter movement. As long as the women's shelter movement does a good job, it will continue to receive funds.

The main component of the official funding program is that up to 50 percent of the costs of start-up and operation will be covered by the central government as long as the local municipality or county municipality will cover the rest. Thus, expansion has followed a decentralized model in which the establishment and operation of the individual shelter have been primarily dependent on the goodwill of the local authorities and not on central government direction. The municipal governments may decide the extent of their funding of shelters within their jurisdiction, and there is no regulation of the number of shelters per resident or geographic density.

The Norwegian Ministry of Health and Social Affairs submitted in 1988 a proposal for hearing that suggested a change in the public funding program to a system of distribution of funds to the county governments based on population, with a provision for the compensation of sparsely populated areas. The shelters were opposed to the proposal and personally contacted the Minister of Health and Social Affairs to express their disagreement. The shelter groups viewed the proposal as an attempt to increase government control over the shelters. Furthermore, they were not in favor of the attempt to develop a better geographic spread within the limitations of the department's budget. The proposed program would necessarily have had a negative effect on the existing shelters in certain counties. The proposal was not passed; this is indicative of the extent to which the women's shelter movement has been legitimized within the political system.

Public Financing Means Tight Budgets, but Weak Public Control

In contrast to the general program for the transfer of funds from central to local government authorities, the funds for the women's shelters are earmarked. The usual practice in such transfers involves so-called "blanket allocations," from which the municipal government may allocate funds as it sees fit within the given limitations. Shelters have thus avoided having to compete with other sectors for the central government funds. The fact that the ministry has guaranteed up to 50 percent of the approved budget has made it easier for municipal governments to commit themselves to financial involvement in the operation of the shelters.

Even so, the greatest limitation for the women's shelters has been their tight budgets, which have particularly affected the principle of full compensation for all volunteer work. There are many shelters that either continually or periodically have had to resort to little or no compensation to maintain a balanced budget. The alternative has been periodic closing while waiting for extra funds to be granted or for the next budget year to begin. In such a situation, most shelters have chosen to remain open, but it seems evident now that more and more shelters are opting for closing part of the year because their funds are inadequate (Jonassen, 1989). This may be an indication that the "pioneer phase" is now over for many women's shelters: They have documented the need for their existence and are no longer willing to give in so easily.

The financial model is that the municipal governments decide the total amount of money given to shelters because central government covers up to 50 percent of what is given by municipal governments. At the central level, decisions in the early 1990s had been very positive for the women's shelters. The budget was almost doubled between 1990 and 1991, from 21,571 million kroner to 41,178 million kroner (including money to the shelters helping incest victims). Furthermore, in 1992, the original budget proposal was changed in two important ways: First, money from central government now covers 50 percent of the total budget, rather than up to 50 percent; second, the central government now covers 50 percent of the money coming from municipal governments and from other givers. The new model really opens up fundraising in the event that in the future women's shelters wish to become more independent of local public financing.

The local variations in the presence of external representatives on the shelters' executive board or other committees represent an adjustment that each shelter has had to make on the basis of local conditions—particularly the need to secure the financial side of operations. Even though this has been relatively unproblematic for most shelters, having a good relationship with a source of funds has required structural adjustments that conflict with original principles (Jonassen, 1989). On the other hand, the design of the program for government funding makes no stipulation about the recipients' daily operations or management. This absence of rules, regulations, or other attempts by the central government to standardize and structure the centers is extremely atypical for programs for which the government provides financial assistance to voluntary organizations (Kuhnle & Selle, 1992b).

Therefore, it can be said that the women's shelter movement has been successful in obtaining public funds for the shelters on its own terms. In Norway publicly funded, voluntarily run help organizations with such a degree of independence are very rare. Even more extraordinary is the fact that the movement grew at a time when "the public sector view" in health and social services was at its strongest. Other social service–help organizations of a partly voluntary, partly public nature are run by older humanitarian organizations, which began their work at a time when government involvement was not as extensive. Even though these other organizations are closer to the public sector in terms of ideology and service production, government control in general is much greater.

No Charity

The women's shelter movement emphasizes that it does not run any form of charity work. The movement is based on the belief that the government has an obligation to provide financing for services for battered women and is consistent with the rights-based principles on which the Norwegian welfare state is built. Public funding is seen as a way to make both the problem and the problem solvers legitimate. The problem of autonomy versus complete dependence on government funds has never been an important topic of discussion, reflecting the strong legitimacy and the openness of the public sector (Kuhnle & Selle, 1992b).

It is unusual that the women's shelter movement chooses to run the shelters itself rather than leave operation to the public sector. The movement has done so because the operation of the shelters has meant much more than simply helping—it represents the women's rights battle in practice. The shelter movement became one of the first specific expressions of self-help: Peers can provide help that is qualitatively different and better than public sector help.

To understand the success of this politicized alternative movement, a main difference between the situation in Norway and in Britain should be emphasized. Pahl (1985) described the difficulty in Britain of being both a charitable organization and a pressure group. To achieve charitable status, a prerequisite for fundraising, an organization may not be political; but that is precisely what shelters are, in that they relate violence against women to deeper structures in society at large. This is a totally unknown problem in Norway. First, Norway has no strong tradition of fundraising for voluntary or charity organizations. Second, private contributors are not allowed tax deductions. Third, public support is not linked to any specific criteria that the organizations must meet.

How Public Responsibility Was Redefined

Despite the dependence on municipal goodwill and the eternal struggle against tight budgets, the women's shelter movement has won its struggle for public funding without further public involvement. It is necessary, however, to take a closer look at the establishment of the program for public funding to understand why the central government relented to such a degree to the demands of the movement—especially considering that the demand for publicly funded, privately run and controlled shelters was controversial because it represented a new form for the welfare service organization and that the fundamental beliefs of the movement made it problematic for some people to accept its demands.

Three public initiatives stand out in connection with the gradual acceptance of the abuse of women as a political issue and the gradual acceptance of the demands made by the women's shelter movement. The first initiative was the support granted by the Ministry of Health and Social Affairs to the two-year trial running of the women's shelter in Oslo in 1978. The second initiative was the formation of the program for government funding in 1982. When the government's "program for action against the abuse of women" was presented in 1983, it was the final affirmation that abuse of women is a serious social problem for which the government has a particular responsibility and that efforts in this area should be channeled through the shelters in their existing form.

Behind these three initiatives was a tug-of-war between the Ministry of Health and Social Affairs on the one hand and the Directorate of Health and the Ministry of Consumer Affairs and Government Administration on the other. The Ministry of Health and Social Affairs considered the abuse of women to be within its jurisdiction but was negative toward the demands of the women's shelter movement. Despite this attitude, the ministry was surprisingly passive; it made no attempt to prepare proposals for the integration of new programs for battered women into the existing system.

The Directorate of Health and the Ministry of Consumer Affairs and Government Administration periodically defined abuse of women as a health- and family-related matter, so they could transfer funds from their budgets for the establishment and operation of shelters whose applications had been rejected by the Ministry of Health and Social Affairs. In this manner, the Ministry of Health and Social Affairs was pressured into granting funds to maintain control over the area of abuse of women. It was in this way that the government program for funding of the shelters came into being in 1982.

At the same time, there was considerable focus on the issue in the media, and there was broad political support in Parliament. As early as 1980, a unanimous Parliamentary Standing Committee on Health and Social

Affairs supported the applications for funds that had been submitted by 13 shelters. Even so, at this time the ministry rejected the applications.

Norway had a Labor Government until 1981. In view of the party's emphasis on the responsibility of the state for national welfare, it is understandable that its members were skeptical about voluntary women's shelters. This skepticism probably was the cause of the ministry's opposition. The political leaders in the Ministry of Consumer Affairs and Government Administration, despite their Labor Party membership, were more positively inclined; whether this was a function of the ministry's having a female leader is difficult to say. In 1981 a Conservative Government took over, and apparently this government had fewer problems in accepting women's shelters as voluntarily run and controlled projects, despite the ideological distance.

The broad support that the women's shelter movement enjoyed resulted from the movement's considerable potential for interpretation. For the conservatives, the movement represented an admirable example of an attempt by volunteers to take the initiative and assume responsibility. The value-conservative Christian Peoples Party considered the movement an important step in the work to protect mother and child. Leftist concern with the question of private versus public responsibility gradually surrendered to the desire to support a specific expression of the women's movement. Furthermore, it was the women's shelter movement that exposed the problem of abuse of women, and shelters were offering the only definite form of help. It was very easy to go along with the shelters, continuing to be the problem solvers on their own terms.

The women's shelter movement has not had centrally placed supporters within the bureaucracy itself, although within the broad spectrum of women's organizations and political parties, there has been wide support. The lack of supporters in the administrative system may be a disadvantage in the future. If issues involving changes in programs for battered women are not raised at the political level but rather are left to the administration of the Ministry of Children and Family Affairs and the Ministry of Health and Social Affairs, the influence of the women's shelter movement will be reduced. Similarly, there is a danger in the decentralized model represented by the funding program. The shelters' existence is determined by the individual municipality. Goodwill on the part of the central authorities will not be of any use if the question of continued operation of the shelters is out of the ministry's hands.

Public funding has limited the activities of the shelter groups in that municipal representatives sit on the executive boards or finance committees, and tight budgets do not allow for compensation of the volunteers. Certain groups also claim that the never-ending financial–practical side of operation has overshadowed the political side. Nevertheless, the women's shelter groups, despite their complete dependence on the public sector for funding, largely have been able to maintain autonomy and control over their product. Will that be true in the near future? Will the movement still have the ideological strength and the service potential to meet the challenges of the 1990s?

Will the 1990s Be a Period of Consolidation?

The Collapse of the "Center"

In October 1989, there was nearly a revolution at the Oslo shelter, the natural "center" and trendsetter within the women's shelter movement. Events there provide a good picture both of the dependence of women's shelters on the goodwill of the municipal government and of the problematic conflict within a flat organizational structure.

Until autumn 1989 the Oslo shelter represented, with its flat structure, the organizational ideal within the movement. Members of this shelter were among the most outspoken opponents of a national organization for women's shelters, and it was this group that most often chose to close its shelters when the allotted funds were not adequate.

This was the situation before the "coup" at the Oslo shelter in 1989. The shelter had been closed for four to five weeks in protest against the proposed budget for 1990. The group had, however, agreed to a new proposal, and the shelter had been reopened when the "bomb" was dropped. A small splinter group had secretly negotiated a takeover of the shelter with Oslo's Municipal Executive Board.

The shock was considerable in many different circles. The model shelter in the movement had collapsed. The media covered the event quite extensively, and it was evident that the conflict ran deep. Those with some knowledge of the shelter knew that there had been disagreements among members in certain areas for quite some time. Differences were evident particularly in such issues as the amount of time and resources that should be spent on incest victims with aftereffects and on immigrant women. The splinter group was of the opinion that incest victims with aftereffects were not in acute crisis and, therefore, should not have access to the shelter. The same group had aired the idea of creating a separate unit for immigrant women, instead of having all women under the same roof. These proposals were made in the context of the capacity problems at the shelter, which at times could be extreme.

The splinter group members also claimed that despite the existence of the general assembly, there was no democracy within the organization, and they felt overridden and manipulated. The original group, on the other hand, was shocked—up until the last general assembly, the new group, which consisted of many of the original group's most central members, supported the shelter's program.

The Municipal Executive Board consisted of a coalition of the Conservative Party and the Progress Party, and it gradually became clear that the takeover was a matter of prestige for the Board's Conservative chair. The original shelter group had broad support: The Oslo chief of police and a group of 90 politicians and prominent researchers in women's studies delivered a protest to the board against its treatment of the matter. Many leading woman politicians in the Conservative Party were included in this group. The original shelter group also interpreted the signals from the Labor Party Minister of Health and Social Affairs as positive; however, she had no authority to intervene in a municipal government matter. In the end, the splinter group was allowed to assume operation of the shelter.

The women's shelter in Oslo is still run by the new group, which, with a few exceptions, consists of newly recruited members. The organizational structure is no longer completely flat but is what the group calls "flat internally and hierarchical externally." This means, among other things, that external contact is channeled through selected representatives. The original shelter group continued to operate a help line until the spring of 1991, when the help line was discontinued. This group's only hope of resuming control of the Oslo shelter was in the municipal elections in the autumn of 1991. They regarded a socialist majority in the City Council as their last chance. Oslo did get a socialist majority, but the original group has by now given up hope of taking back the shelter.

It is evident now that if a powerful national umbrella organization had existed, the splinter group's influence would have been far more limited. Similarly, the takeover indicates the disadvantages of being totally dependent on public funding. Local government became part of a political play caused by internal conflict within the shelter movement and, therefore, had a strong influence on the outcome. However, it should be emphasized that government could not have intervened or become involved without deep conflict within the movement.

Will the Future Be Different?

The women's shelter movement is characterized by greater heterogeneity than the common platform might suggest. The percentage of politically active women probably has declined, while the percentage of women who are primarily motivated by a general desire to help has increased. Nevertheless, there have been developments during the last few years that indicate that the movement has not lost all its original fire. At the national conference in 1990, the original shelter group from Oslo received unconditional backing through the passage of a declaration of support; this occurred without any form of lobbying. The present shelter group, on the other hand, was the subject of considerable criticism.

Within the women's shelter movement, there has been considerable fear that the ministry will decide that the shelters should be run by municipal governments. There are at present two such government-run shelters. All staff are permanently employed at these shelters, and they are trained either in health care and social services or in other therapist-related areas. These shelters are run much the same as other municipal institutions. One of these shelters in particular has been critical of the fact that it has not been allowed to join the women's shelter movement, and it is feared that these two shelters are in the process of lobbying the ministry for the introduction of their model on a national basis.

In the spring of 1991, the two government-run shelters formed the Norwegian Women's Shelter Movement (Norsk Krisesenterbevegelse), which was to be a national organization for all shelters. Help lines were not included, and thus the old shelter group from Oslo was excluded from this organization. Bylaws and organizational guidelines already had been prepared when the membership invitations were sent out. Two of the shelters within the orignal movement reacted immediately and called an extraordinary national conference to discuss the development. The unanimous conclusion was that the invitation to join the organization should be refused. Thus, the new organization consists of only those few groups that were already outside the women's shelter movement. A few other shelters have become members of the new organization, but the great majority are still members of the original national group. The "new" women's shelter in Oslo is not part of either of the two national organizations but is autonomous. There is extensive organizational uncertainty, which could result in comprehensive organizational change in the near future.

Despite the potential organizational and ideological changes, the women's shelter movement can be said to have succeeded in its work thus far. It managed to put abuse of women on the public agenda, and it won the battle to run shelters on its own terms with public funds. The movement has had to deviate from the principle of full compensation because of tight budgets, but there is no reason to believe that it has become more charity-oriented over the years. The shelters have, with few exceptions, moved away from the purely flat organizational structure. The current hierarchical or semihierarchical organizational structures may be seen partly as a result of the necessity of adjusting to financial contributors, but they also reflect the heterogeneous membership's varying views on the significance of organizational structure.

Although its ideological overtones are not as noticeable as they were in the early 1980s, the women's shelter movement still seems capable of both survival and action. Along the way, the members have become less expressive and more instrumentally oriented; however, the political features are still present. The movement has a long way to go before it becomes like any other social service. In addition to operating the shelters, the members also work to spread information regarding their activities and abuse of women in general. It is in this specific area of dissemination that everyone agrees some form of national organization would be helpful. However, there is a growing majority that considers the time ripe for a more permanent national organization—to secure the shelters in their existing form so that they will be better able to withstand pressure both from within and without.

The women's shelter movement seems to be heading toward existence as an interest and self-help organization. If the movement survives this transition without splitting apart, it will probably be in a better position to protect its financial interests with central and local government. At the same time, however, it will have moved even further from its original value foundation.

Conclusion: What Does the Women's Shelter Represent?

The women's shelter movement provides almost perfect insight into the essence of being an alternative movement in a state-friendly society. In Norway, it is unusual for alternative movements to turn away from the state; more commonly, they turn toward it, particularly those in service production. As a consequence, most problems end up becoming a public responsibility. People are of the opinion that they have a right to public funds to straighten things out. The state should finance and the organization should produce—with state guarantees should anything go wrong. At the same time, state control must not be too great. It may be that a commingling of the public and private sectors is becoming more acceptable. It appears that the public sector is increasingly opting for public financing in combination with private production and control, a result of neoliberal ideas that have influenced even the most state-oriented welfare states (Selle, 1993).

In the ideological climate that has emerged after the breakdown of the hierarchical and rather centralized management model in the 1980s, we have seen the introduction of comprehensive modernization plans for the public sector in all Scandinavian countries (Olsen, 1988). These programs emphasize decentralized and user-oriented solutions and also aim at giving the market and the voluntary sector a larger role. The increasing legitimacy of the voluntary sector (and the market) could result in an increased service role and a more comprehensive ideological space for the voluntary sector, that is, the new welfare pluralism (Kuhnle & Selle, 1990, 1992b; Selle, 1993). Of great interest is that the women's shelter movement pushed through such a model even before the neoliberal ideas really started to influence public policy.

In a study of the development of the relationship between the public sector and voluntary organizations, it was evident that although it was not uncommon for the public sector to take over former voluntary organizations' service production, this did not always happen. And such takeovers did not make voluntary organizations superfluous. There is no empirical support for the suggestion that voluntary organizations that initiated the provision of new services were later taken over by force. The voluntary organizations, and particularly those in service production, were integrated into public policy quite early, and the organizations themselves often served as the impetus for public takeover. The organizations looked for public rather than private alternatives as early as the turn of the century (Kuhnle & Selle 1990, 1992b).

On the basis of this general historical review and the current ideological climate, the probability of the public sector assuming responsibility for the shelters' work by force must be considered minimal. However, it is important to note that should the shelter movement be unable to continue its extensive service production in the abuse of women, the public sector would be forced to build public institutions of one form or another, because the women's shelter movement has made abuse of women a public problem.

One reason it is so difficult for state-friendly societies to argue against public grants for movements that originally are quite removed from the ideology and organizational form of the welfare state has to do with the question of rights. This is true in general, but particularly true in service provision. Once abuse of women was accepted as a public matter, it was no longer a question of the rights of the members of the movement but of the rights of the battered women. It is difficult, if not impossible, to argue that these women do not have a right to help. When service providers are found who take such groups seriously, it is difficult to argue against grants to these organizations—even if one does not agree with their ideology. This is particularly the case if the groups do a good job, indeed, a better job than it is believed a new public sector service would do.

What, in addition to the connection between the women's shelter movement and the public sector, makes the movement seem both deviant and modern? Its emphasis is on decentralization and user orientation, which corresponds with developmental features in public policy in general. Thus, the movement can be seen as part of a growing pluralistic culture resulting from a gradual breakdown in the belief in hierarchy—a culture in which all paternalistic structures will be broken. Both ideologically and organizationally, more egalitarian values are developed, involving a deemphasizing of the professional orientation of the modern welfare state (Ellis, Thompson, & Wildavsky, 1990; Inglehart, 1989).

Nevertheless, it is obvious that the women's shelter movement has problems today concerning objectives, ideology, and organizational form. It is also evident that there are somewhat sizable differences of opinion inherent in the organization. There appears to be a relatively strong shift in the direction of being a source of help and away from being a form of political action. This may be more a result of internal processes within the feminist movement in general, and in the women's shelter movement in particular, than of public influence resulting from the program for public funding. The shift is primarily a result of the fact that the women's movement, of which the women's shelter movement is an important part, lost much of its force in the 1980s. This development strengthened the more service oriented in the organization and probably altered the frame of reference for the ideology-oriented political activists. A weakened women's movement makes it far more difficult to legitimize considerable emphasis on women's policy and ideology as integrated parts of service production.

Public funding may have influenced the internal relationships in the movement in that it strengthened the position of the most service-oriented members. Nevertheless, this should not be overdramatized. It was during the period in which the ideology-oriented members were dominant that the special relationship with the public sector was developed. At that time, the women's shelter movement was a highly politicized alternative movement—indeed, a form of political action. The movement was able to negotiate public funding because as a voluntary organization it was able to make the social problem with which it was concerned visible to the public. In other words, movement members made their problem a public problem. And the movement succeeded in this goal without reducing the ideological distance between itself and the public sector.

Thus the most important difference from the past is that the public sector now increasingly accepts more private control of public problems, whereas, at the same time, the women's shelter movement has become less distant ideologically. Comprehensive change in public policy and goal displacement within the women's shelter movement imply that the relationship between the women's shelter movement and government increasingly grows normal.

It has never been easy to be an alternative movement in a state-friendly society. What seems to be rather easy, and probably much easier than in less state-friendly societies, is influencing public policies. However, in doing so the alternative movement does not stay the same. That is true whether it is part of the women's movement or part of any other organization on the fringe.

References

Alsaksen, I. (1979). "Camilla," Krisesenteret for voldtatte og mishandlede kvinner. *Hefte for Kritisk Juss, 3*(4), 19–25.

Alsaksen, I., & Nisja, R. (1980). *Krisesenteret for voldtatte mishandlede kvinner [The women's shelter movement]*. INAS-rapport 80/2. Oslo, Norway.

Barne-og familiestatistikk: Statistikk-Krisetiltak, 1991 [Children and family statistics: Statistics and Emergency Act, 1991]. Oslo, Norway: Barne-og Familiedepartementet.

Bleiklie, I. (1980). *Forskning for svaktstiltes forhold til forvaltningen [Research on weak groups' relationships toward the public sector]*. Arbeids rapport [Working report], Forvaltningen og svaktstilte brukere, 80/1 Bergen: University of Bergen.

Ellis, R., Thompson, M., & Wildavsky, A. (1990). *Cultural theory*. Boulder, CO: Westview Press.

Freeman, M. D. A. (1987). Violence against women; does the legal system provide solutions, or does itself constitute the problem? *British Journal of Law and Society, 7*, 215–241.

Haukaa, R. (1982). *Bak slagordene [Behind the slogans]*. Oslo, Norway: Pax Forlag.

Inglehart, R. (1989). *Cultural change in advanced industrial society*. Princeton, NJ: Princeton University Press.

Jonassen, W. (1987). *Vennetjeneste eller offentlig tiltak? En analyse av organisering og drift av krisesentrene [Act of friendship or public untaking. An analysis of the organization and the management of the women's shelters]*. NIBR-rapport 87/10. Oslo, Norway.

Jonassen, W. (1989). *Kvinner hjelper kvinner [Women help women]*. NIBR-rapport 89/4. Oslo, Norway.

Kuhnle, S. (1983). *Velferdsstatens utvikling [The development of the welfare state]*. Bergen, Norway: Universitetsforlaget.

Kuhnle, S. (1990, April). *The Scandinavian welfare model in the era of European integration*. Paper presented at ECPR Planning Session, Ruhr Universität, Bochum, Germany.

Kuhnle, S., & Selle, P. (1990). Meeting needs in a welfare state: Relations between government and voluntary organizations in Norway. In

degrees in many western European nations (Henshaw & Tietze, 1986). It was not until 1973 that the prohibition against abortion in the United States was eliminated with *Roe v. Wade*, which ruled that "a woman's constitutional right to privacy includes her right to decide, in consultation with her physician, whether or not to terminate her pregnancy" (Gold, l990, p. 1). Until then a dual system of care existed: a limited class of women with means could travel abroad or to selected states to have abortions performed, albeit at great sacrifice; however, most women were unable to afford this luxury. Consequently, less affluent women were forced to resort to desperate measures, often having illegal abortions at great personal risk. Thus, as late as l965, 17 percent of all deaths related to pregnancy and childbirth resulted from illegal abortions, and the mortality rate for minority women was 12 times that of white women (Cates & Rochat, l976). As a result of this dramatic problem, a social movement developed that focused on abortions as a critical need to be addressed.

At the same time, the women's movement had begun, with a focus on empowerment, self-help, and political action. It served as a major force for change in the 1960s and 1970s. One of the spinoffs of the broader women's movement was the development of a new health system, composed of alternative organizations seeking to meet women's health needs.

A series of events in the early l970s had sparked the birth of the women's health movement. These included the emergence of gynecological self-help groups, the publication of a monthly women's health movement newsletter, a women's health conference in New York, and the opening of several feminist health centers (Thomas, l993). Perhaps the most important precipitating event was the legalization of abortion on the national level. Ruzek (1978) reported that by the mid-l970s, there were more than 100 women's health organizations in the United States. These organizations shared a philosophy that reflected a radical commitment to "service and structure" as they focused on the need for social change, both to get at the root of social problems they sought to redress and to alleviate internal organizational problems (Thomas, 1993).

The radical commitment of these organizations played itself out in interesting ways. As advocates, their ideological orientations facilitated their involvement in political action; as feminists, their ideological orientations committed them to participatory democracy and to nonbureaucratic organizational structures. Their struggles with both external and internal constraints are exemplified in the developmental history presented in this chapter—the case study of the Elizabeth Blackwell Health Center for Women.

With the election of President Reagan in l980, the social climate began to change as the antiabortion forces became vocal in their opposition to *Roe v. Wade*. Despite a 1975 National Academy of Sciences report suggesting that legal abortions involve less morbidity and mortality than illegal abortions, in 1987 Reagan directed his Surgeon General, Dr. C. Everett Koop, to issue another report that would detail the negative consequences of abortion and reflect a conservative view. However, Dr. Koop's report of findings after a 15-month study differed from what the President had expected or wanted. The report stated that any psychological trauma caused by an abortion was "miniscule from a public health perspective and that accompanying pregnancy-related problems were not more frequent among women who had abortions than those who did not" (Gold, 1990, p. 9). Nevertheless, the counterforces were increasing and many states and the federal government sought to mount restrictions in various ways: The use of public money, including Medicaid funds, to pay for abortions was prohibited in 1980 in *Harris v. McRae*; in 1989, sharply limiting *Roe v. Wade*, the Supreme Court ruled that states could impose a range of restrictions on abortion (*Webster v. Reproductive Health Services*).

In addition to the increasing political and legal opposition, in the social arena dramatic changes occurred as antichoice–antiabortion forces increasingly mounted protests and demonstrations at many of the women's health facilities. There were increasing threats and violence—property was destroyed and a physician who worked in an abortion facility was murdered. Thus, as a result of a dramatically changing external environment since the 1980s, many of the women's health organizations have had to deal with a variety of threats to their survival.

Women's Health Movement

The growing literature on the women's health movement highlights the radical departure from conventional health services of the organizations established to serve the special needs of women (Stern, 1986). The literature also provides insight into the forces that led to the 1974 founding of the Elizabeth Blackwell Health Center for Women in Philadelphia. It is important to articulate the critical issues that all women's health organizations face and that served to stimulate the development of this significant segment of activity in the women's movement. All the issues are equally important and affected the creation of a definition of mission, policy formation, priority setting, and implementation.

First was the concern with meeting the specific health needs of women that the broader health system was not addressing. Initially, the primary concern was the ability of women to obtain abortions under safe and sanitary conditions.

The second issue addressed the philosophy of patient care. All too often, women were treated as objects in the medical establishment—a demeaning situation. The emphasis here was on women as consumers or clients, with the implication that they would be actively involved in the decision-making process regarding their own bodies.

Third, and directly related to the second issue, was the concept of empowerment, a focus of the broader women's movement, including decision making related not only to individual patient care but also to services that were needed by women in general. This concept affected the planning and design of services to meet the unique gender-related needs, including gynecological examinations, menopausal services, and preventive educational programs.

The fourth issue involved commitment to advocacy and systems change. All of the women's health organizations were committed to a dual mission: providing service and impacting broader social policy.

Fifth and last was the commitment to the feminist value of the participatory management–participatory democracy concept of organizational governance. Thus, a hierarchically run organization was antithetical to these women's organizations (Ferguson, 1984).

Although these nontraditional organizations often did not survive and although many of those that did survive became increasingly traditional in both outlook and structure (Thomas, 1993), several not only have survived but also have remained committed to social change goals and principles (Metzendorf, 1990). The Elizabeth Blackwell Health Center for Women is such an organization.

Each of the above issues dealt with in the case study of the Elizabeth Blackwell Health Center for Women. The organizational dilemmas that were created as the center was challenged to grow and change in order to survive—as well as the resolution of these dilemmas—will be considered. The analysis focuses on power and decision making within this alternative agency.

Case Study

The issues the women's health organizations face highlight their radical departure from conventional health services and also provide insight into the forces that led to the founding of the Elizabeth Blackwell Health Center for Women. This feminist agency has made many critical decisions over its almost two decades of existence that not only created but also sustained an unconventional management style, while simultaneously protecting its survival. The following discussion is organized around a series of critical organizational variables, including mission, policy-making and governance, financial resources, human resources, and programs.

Organizational Beginnings

Defining the Mission

The Elizabeth Blackwell Health Center for Women was organized in the summer of 1974 by a group of women who saw a need for nonprofit, women-controlled abortion services. The group came together out of a common negative work experience in a commercially financed, physician-owned, for-profit abortion facility.

It was clear to the center's founders that the quality of services provided to women is affected by the ownership, philosophy, and goals of the organization. These women drew on the experience of other women around the country who were already involved in self-help clinics and study groups. The group sought to apply these experiences to their local community, Philadelphia—a large urban area with an extensive, sophisticated, and fairly traditional medical system.

Guided by the values and issues discussed earlier, the founders determined to organize a health center that would provide high-quality, low-cost health services to all women in a democratic environment of respect for each person and maximal participation by consumers and staff (Elizabeth Blackwell Health Center for Women, *Statement of Principles*, 1975). During 14 months of planning, the founders made a series of critical decisions that implemented the principles articulated above and that were to govern the organization:

- The fee-generating services made self-sufficiency and continuity realistic goals, because fees allowed a degree of freedom that would be impossible with complete dependence on grants. Thus, fiscal accountability and fiscal viability were realistic goals from the onset.

- Start-up funding would not come from an individual or a group of individuals who could subsequently, either subtly or overtly, control the organization.

- The organization would be a nonprofit corporation. Its board of directors, elected by consumers, would be composed of interested individuals—primarily women—who could lend expertise and advice to the center.

- Staff would have maximum access to information and decision making, short of being a collective. This access would be accomplished, in part, by requiring that one third of the board of directors be staff-elected staff members and that all board committees include staff representatives (Elizabeth Blackwell Health Center for Women, *By-Laws*, 1976).

- The organization would seek to limit the traditional disparities of salary and power among staff, although there would be specific and distinct job titles and descriptions, and the salaries would vary.

- The women to be served would be called "consumers," in an effort to enhance their power in relationships with the service providers at the center and in contrast to the connotation of powerlessness inherent in the term "patient." Consumers would be sought from a widely diverse population; the center was committed from the outset to serving women of all income levels, ages, racial and ethnic backgrounds, and lifestyles—including lesbians, as well as heterosexual women who had never identified themselves as feminists.

- Because an initial goal was to provide services to "women like ourselves," the staff and board would be representative of the race, age, experience, and lifestyles of the women who were to be served and would provide services they themselves would wish to use.

- Abortion and contraceptive services would be offered within the context of complete "well-woman" gynecological care.

- The center would use what was valuable in the traditional health care system and, at the same time, seek to expand on that system and to challenge its inequities for both worker and consumer.

The philosophies of self-help and participatory health care were incorporated to ensure that each woman's experience was validated and that women sharing with each other would augment the strength and knowledge of all involved (Elizabeth Blackwell Health Center for Women, *Statement of Principles*, 1975).

In addition, the founders made a critical decision in terms of organizational mission not to accept any public funding for the center's programs. This provision was made to ensure the autonomy and independence of the organization (Perlmutter, 1971).

Program Implementation

The center opened in October 1975, with a staff and board integrated by race, class, ethnicity, age, and education, the board being somewhat more middle-class, well educated, and professional than the staff. The women involved with the center identified themselves as feminists, but most had not worked in alternative organizations and, therefore, had little experience in either collective or self-help groups. The director was a professional with experience in a consumer-oriented health care delivery system. She also was one of the founders and was strongly committed to the feminist goals and philosophy of the organization.

In its first decade, the center grew dramatically. Between 1976 and 1986, the annual budget increased from $220,000 to $800,000; services increased from 5,000 visits to more than 10,000 visits; personnel expanded from eight to 35 full- and part-time staff, from 12 to 40 volunteers and students, and from a 15- to a 21-member board of directors. Funding sources remained fairly consistent, with approximately 80 percent of funds generated through fees for services and 20 percent from foundation grants and private donations. Except for the one and only small grant using public funds—$2,500 from the U.S. Department of Health, Education and Welfare in 1976 for a cancer screening program—there was no further direct government funding of the center.

The following discussion focuses on power and decision making at the Blackwell Center, as reflected in policy and governance, personnel, and services. Although these three dimensions are highly interrelated in this agency, for purposes of analysis they will be treated separately.

Policy-making, Planning, and Governance

The issue of power arises in both obvious and subtle ways in all organizations. Some members of alternative organizations are reluctant to acknowledge the importance of authority and power as instrumental in defining relationships and as a functional imperative to accomplishing an organization's movement toward its goals. At the Blackwell Center there was, from the beginning, an effort to accept the appropriate contribution of leadership and authority and, at the same time, to recognize the importance of each staff member's contribution.

Equally important, however, was the establishment of a system of checks and balances to limit the accumulation of power. This was accomplished both by ensuring accountability of the individual to the whole group (either to the entire staff or the board of directors) and by devising mechanisms that contributed to the intricate and perhaps unique balance struck between hierarchy and collective structure. This hybrid structure, while complex at times, has enabled the organization to accomplish its goals, to grow, and to change, while remaining committed to its initial feminist philosophy.

Initially, although each staff member had a specific job description, there was considerable flexibility and job rotation. As the organization matured and the staff grew in number, this flexibility diminished; staff members were less likely to carry responsibilities or perform tasks unrelated to their own specific jobs. Nonetheless, significant time and energy were devoted to including all staff in problem solving and decision making. For example, all staff members had the opportunity to serve on board committees and attend board meetings.

Considerable attention also was given to creating mechanisms by which all levels of staff could respond to issues that affect the organization. The administrative staff ensured that information was shared by having all staff members understand the issues, consider options, voice opinions, and arrive at agreement on the direction to take. However, it should be noted that interest in and ability to share decision-making authority required ongoing staff education, because most new staff brought with them the attitudes of powerlessness inherent in most traditional workplaces and had to be informed of the mechanisms available for direct involvement in decision making.

Staff's willingness to speak openly about policy issues and to consider the larger impact on the organization, as well as their own positions on an issue, were some of the positive aspects of their shared commitment to relate to each other collectively. But this process was also difficult and required active and conscious commitment.

The collective process also was used to modify existing programs and plan for new ones. Ideas for new programs were generated informally by staff throughout the year and by the board in its annual long-range planning process, in which goals and objectives for the year were delineated in detail. This process pushed the center to plan concretely for the following year and also to consider goals for several years ahead. There was increasing pressure from the board to develop a five-year plan for the center, and consequently, a long-range planning committee was formed. This formalization of the planning process was intended to increase the Blackwell Center's flexibility and responsiveness to community needs.

Personnel

Staff relationships at the Blackwell Center reflected not only the principles articulated above but also the informality that is possible in a small organization. At the inception of the agency, staff reported to the executive director or the assistant director and rejected additional levels of hierarchy. Over time, the agency grew more complex as it added staff, diversified services, and delineated staff roles more precisely. To accommodate this growth, some staff began to assume informal supervisory roles with students, volunteers, and other staff. This informal supervision led to the need for clarification of responsibilities and identification of appropriate levels of supervision. The board and staff agreed to recognize and legitimize certain lines of accountability that were already operational; consequently, roles were more clearly delineated and other lines of accountability were clarified. These refinements did not change the basic structure, in which all staff had access to information and decision making.

Other key areas of decision making included hiring and firing, staff evaluations, and salary. These were areas that most severely challenged ability of staff members to see beyond their own personal needs and to focus on organizational needs. Hiring and firing of all staff except the executive director was the responsibility of a committee whose membership was rotated among all staff on a quarterly basis. This committee also decided on the salaries to be paid to new staff, within ranges set by a board committee. Both the executive director and staff members, through their membership on the board, were thus involved in this process, illustrating the blend of traditional (the board hiring the executive director and setting salary ranges) and alternative (the staff hiring each other) organizational models.

With regard to evaluations, all staff members were evaluated annually by all others. These written performance evaluations were reviewed with the staff members and the executive and assistant directors. Unsatisfactory evaluations were brought before the staff committee for formal review and determination. On occasion, staff members were put on probation or even fired by this committee, in a process both lengthy and painful.

Salary decisions also were viewed in relation to the Blackwell Center's organizing principles, which attempted to deal with problems of distributive justice. The matter of salary disparity became a prominent issue as the organization grew and became more professionalized. Several factors led to the increasing disparity in salaries: the longevity of some staff, changes in job descriptions, and the addition of staff with advanced professional training.

One means by which to deal with disparities was a mechanism the board and staff developed to determine salary increases. Before this time (1982), there were either no increases or "across-the-board" increases. After much discussion, it was decided that staff members would receive a set increase on the anniversary date of employment—the amount, $300 to $500, based on the number of years employed at the center. In addition, the board would grant an annual cost-of-living increase if the center's financial situation permitted: In the odd years, this would be a percentage of each staff person's salary; in the even years, it would be a percentage of the median salary, meaning a smaller increase in the higher salary range and a larger increase at the lower end of the salary range. In this way, the disparity issue was addressed at least in part. Although there was some grumbling, most of the staff members became committed to this concept.

Services

From the outset, the Blackwell Center offered a wide range of women's health care services, including contraception, pregnancy testing, options counseling, and abortion services. In addition, the center provided gynecological care for women past childbearing age. Over time, the center expanded its services to full maternity care, including an out-of-hospital birth center staffed by certified nurse-midwives, performance of early second-trimester abortions, insemination of fertile women, anonymous testing for the human immunodeficiency (HIV) virus, and educational programs on menopause, hysterectomy, fertility awareness, nutrition, and childbearing options. Unfortunately, because of a lack of staffing, the out-of-hospital birth center closed in 1989 after five years of operation.

During this first decade, the center continued to advocate politically for women's rights, including access to health care and control over reproductive decisions. The center's health education programs (for example, its workshops) also focused on self-help and consumer rights.

Although new services could always be added in response to consumer interest and staff–board perceptions, a clear and defined means of evaluating these perceptions was never established. Trial and error was the method of expediency, if not choice. One example of the process is demonstrated by the addition of the controversial donor insemination service in 1982. The director and some staff members had become aware that two other women's health centers in the northeastern United States were offering donor insemination. In response to some local interest, discussion was initiated at staff meetings. This idea was further encouraged by board interest in initiating a service for fertile women (primarily lesbians or single heterosexual women) who were unable to conceive for social reasons. The idea was approved by the board, and planning proceeded.

However, when director informally announced the intention to offer the insemination service in the monthly newsletter, the staff unexpectedly raised serious concerns about their own expertise in this area and about the decision to offer this service. Their ambivalence may have reflected the dichotomy identified by Clark (1956), in which he suggested that new, risk-taking programs often reflect "precarious" values, as opposed to the "secure" values of more readily acceptable programs.

In response to staff concerns, two board members led a discussion that focused on the unarticulated issues of the insemination service. Some of the staff's concern had to do with the expectation that they, who had been trained not to be judgmental about women's reproductive decisions, might have to make judgments about who should or should not become a mother. The discussion was helpful and resulted in a clear affirmation of the staff's feelings about helping women to carry out their reproductive options. Assurances were made regarding the importance of obtaining relevant medical and legal advice and of identifying certain contraindications, such as alcoholism and drug addiction, through professional training. Staff members committed themselves to learning what was necessary to offer a high-quality service, and the issue turned out to be a positive learning experience for the entire organization.

The experience confirmed the importance of obtaining staff consensus, based on adequate information and involvement, before initiating a new service or program. Accordingly, the expansion of services in other areas (such as gynecological services for physically disabled and mentally retarded women) was introduced only after a solid foundation of support was laid with both staff and board.

The Blackwell Center is an agency that, in its early stage of organizational development, successfully applied its principles and philosophy to an expanding service, growing staff, and changing times. It remained committed to its original goals but was willing to modify the mechanisms used to achieve them. It took what was valuable from more traditional systems and adapted it to meet the center's need for innovative ways of providing services and managing an organization. This required a vision of what the agency should be, a consistent commitment to the organizational goals, and a willingness to look at itself.

Organizational Strategies for Survival

The second decade following the founding of the Blackwell Center was a period of *Sturm und Drang*. As discussed earlier, the political environment shifted dramatically, as antichoice forces threatened women's health services not only on a legal basis but with physical violence. Abortions now were available in only 17 percent of the counties in the United States. State legislation was enacted to sharply curtail the performance of abortion, with Pennsylvania in the lead. This inhospitable environment pushed to the fore an array of critical problems that the center had to address, especially with regard to the abortion service.

First, whereas the abortion service had supported itself in earlier years and had even been a money raiser for the agency, its income and the resultant profit had decreased as a result of a drop in the potential pool of women in need of this service, the necessity of using volunteers to serve as escorts when protesters threatened the premises—a costly use of resources, the unavailability of doctors to perform abortions because they were fearful about the repercussions of providing this service, and the use of the volunteer telephone counselors to explain which services were available under the restrictive Pennsylvania abortion legislation. In addition, there was increased competition from other nearby providers.

Other stresses included the limited funds available just as the center was trying to expand its gynecological service. This service was not a self-supporting operation: Each gynecological visit required agency subsidy. Because foundations were now under pressure from competing demands, less money was available from a major fiscal resource.

And finally, a new pool of staff and board members had replaced some of the original participants and were questioning many aspects of the center. For example, a board member with expertise in health maintenance organizations (HMOs) raised the issue of the center's segregation from the broader health care delivery system and its inability to care for HMO patients. This situation was caused by the fact that the staff physician was a family practice physician; for HMO coverage, she needed to be a gynecologist. All of these factors precipitated careful soul-searching and planning as the Blackwell Center entered a more mature phase of organizational development. Accordingly, and again reflecting clarity regarding ideological commitments and organizational needs, changes were made.

Reaffirming the Mission

The story of the Blackwell Center is an important one because it illustrates an effective strategy for survival that protected and retained its original mission. This strategy was clearly articulated in the center's new mission statement of 1993, a statement made stronger by its reaffirmation of its founding commitments to advocacy and systems change. Any changes were ones of emphasis, rather than negation. Thus, for example, although specific expertise may now be sought on the board, volunteer, and staff levels, commitment to the center's mission remains a requirement in its new mission statement (Elizabeth Blackwell Health Center, 1993).

> The Elizabeth Blackwell Health Center for Women is founded to provide feminist women's health services and women's health advocacy. The Center is committed to providing high quality, accessible health services for all women regardless of age, race, religion, national origin, marital status, sexual orientation and physical ability, in a setting that enables women to be active participants in their health care. The Center believes that advocacy both for individual women and women's health care issues is essential for creating a just health care system (Elizabeth Blackwell Health Center for Women, 1993)

Some critical decisions have been made regarding the mission, as the organization has sought to merge its ideological commitments with fiscal realities. Whereas in the past there had been no accountability for advocacy activity and only the clinical services (such as abortions and counseling) were tracked in the monthly statistical reports, the approach has been changed to reflect and track education–advocacy activity. The agency retains its commitment not to accept public money.

Program Implementation

The tensions and pressures exerted on the Blackwell Center are reflected in several ways in its implementation of programs. Table 1 indicates the volatility in consumer use of services over a seven-year period.

It should be noted that in 1990 and 1991 the gynecological service, which provided care three days a week, consisted of the family practice physician and two nurse-practitioners. In 1992 and 1993 the nurse-practitioner time was reduced to one nurse-practitioner two days a week. The pregnancy testing service was decreased from two evenings a week in 1990 and 1991 to one evening a week in 1992 and 1993.

The financial data also reflect the center's volatility and vulnerability. Whereas in 1986 the annual budget was $800,000, a steady upward growth did not occur: Although the budget did top the million dollar mark ($1,005,609) in 1991, in 1992 it was down to $943,381 and did not even keep pace with the increased cost of living. However, even in this period of fiscal threat, the agency has continued to refrain from seeking government funding so as to retain its much-cherished autonomy. As in the first stage of the center's development, most of its income is from fees for service (85 percent in 1993 compared with 80 percent in 1986) and the balance comes from private foundations and donations. A more aggressive outreach program is currently planned to obtain non-fee dollars, with initiatives for seeking corporate funding, conducting a membership drive, and exploring the potential revenues from a wellness model of care.

Policy-making and Governance

The basic participatory structure of the board of directors has been retained. This is a critical decision, because one of the major splits in the women's health system has been in the governance model. Many of these health organizations have changed to a corporate model, in which the executive is the only link with the board, and the board consists of high-status corporate members who not only are less committed to a feminist agenda but also are less committed to advocacy. As indicated in Table 2,

Table 1

Organizational Service Statistics

TYPE OF SERVICE	1986	1990-1991	1992-1993
Abortion	1,977	2,170	1,917
Gynecological	4,223	5,314	2,587
Pregnancy testing	1,971	1,305	724

Table 2

Composition of Board of Directors

	NUMBER OF MEMBERS
Community	10
Staff	7
Consumers	3
Total	20

one-third of the Blackwell Center Board still consists of staff members and one of the staff positions is designated as a volunteer's slot.

It should be pointed out, however, that in addition to an ideological commitment on the part of the community-based members, another criterion for nomination to the board is possessing technical skills, such as marketing, management, tax, or law. This dual thrust is necessary in the center's struggle to survive in an inhospitable environment and at the same time retain its unique character. It should also be noted that the center continues to hold the view that although female leadership is a commitment of the organization and the board is composed primarily of women, men are not to be excluded from the board.

There has been a basic change, however, in the governance/leadership approach: A new management team consists of the executive director; the assistant director; the medical director, who is the family practice physician; and two program coordinators. The team is a participatory, policy-making team that meets weekly; it is not an advisory group. Thus, an additional level has been created and some hierarchical features added to the organizational structure, but care to protect staff involvement remains a priority and is being accomplished through the coordinators to whom each staff member reports.

Personnel

There have been important changes in the human resources arena for many reasons. Only the critical changes are highlighted here.

To begin with is the issue of salary. Even in the first stage of organizational development, there was a need to deal with staff pay differences and to handle the disparities. This problem continues to be a major challenge because it is necessary to be competitive with other agencies to attract competent staff. This is particularly true in the health arena and, accordingly, the health professionals are paid more than the social service professionals, and the full-time physician earns more than the executive director. The agency continues to struggle with the equity issue and has continued the formula of odd-and-even–year percentage increases discussed earlier.

Second, as in the other health centers in Metzendorf's (1990) study, there has been a definite move toward *professionalization* and away from a predominantly social movement orientation. Whereas in the early days ideological orientations were key but not exclusive considerations in leadership roles, current realities require a sophisticated organization and a sophisticated leadership coupled with ideological commitments. It should be noted that although there is an attempt to make salaries competitive at all levels of staff, from the executive director to the receptionist, if the staff members were in the for-profit world they would command higher salaries.

Third, the use of *volunteers* now will be more strategically planned, because people will be sought for their specific technical competence. For example, volunteers will be used for public relations, producing the newsletter, marketing, and fundraising.

Despite these changes, what is most impressive about the personnel arrangements in the center is the *longevity* of its key staff. The assistant director has been with the organization since its inception, the rest of the management team for more than 13 years, and a health technician for 14 years. These women are carriers of the history and philosophy of the Blackwell Center!

Services

The most dramatic changes have taken place in the service arena. The center has expanded its purview from a gynecological and reproductive health care focus to a primary health care service meeting all health care needs of women. This has been a critical decision that not only entails broadening the center's service portfolio, but also its organizational relationships. The center has affiliated itself with Graduate Hospital so as to provide its consumers with continuity of care. The center's half-time physician is also medical director of the women's program at Graduate Hospital and serves an important link between the two facilities.

In introducing this new program to the public, emphasis is given to the center's unique approach to health care that empowers consumers to be informed and to make intelligent decisions about their care. In addition to clinical programs, the Blackwell Center also will emphasize preventive care—"a wellness approach."

A second critical decision, and one that was very difficult to make, was closing the out-of-hospital birth center. This full-range service was not viable economically because the number of users was very low and the operation costs very high. In this case, the business side of the enterprise took ascendancy over the ideological commitments. However, the center continues to offer maternity services, with midwives seeing women at the center and the babies delivered, once again, in a hospital.

Third, a critical decision was made to strengthen the gynecological services available to women with special needs related to physical or mental disabilities. A two-year grant from the Pew Foundation has stabilized this service, which now is viewed as a priority and serves primarily a medical assistance (Medicaid) population. Unfortunately, Medicaid pays for only one visit, whereas most of these consumers require three visits. The center's commitment to quality care has created another drain on the budget.

Fourth, the abortion service is still a central program and meticulously follows the letter of the Pennsylvania law, which is becoming increasingly restrictive. It should be noted that although one-third of the abortions performed by the center are covered by HMO contracts and 20 percent are paid for by Blue Cross/Blue Shield and other private insurance companies, the rest are paid for in cash by uninsured women. This places a great burden on the lower income consumers.

Finally, it must be emphasized that the center continues to view advocacy and social change as an integrated part of its work. Each of its services is supported by a broader systems strategy, as evidenced in public meetings, lobbying, and client education.

Summary and Implications

The Elizabeth Blackwell Health Center for Women is an agency that successfully has applied its principles and philosophy to an expanding service, growing staff, and changing times. It remains committed to its original goals but has been willing to modify the mechanisms used to achieve them. It continues to take what is valuable from more traditional systems and channel it into innovative ways of providing services and managing an organization. This requires a vision of what the agency should be, a consistent commitment to the organizational goals, and a willingness to look at itself.

The center has remained in touch with a network of feminist health providers in other areas of the country with whom it discusses ideas and issues, as well as with a group of other feminist organizations in the city that offer interaction and support. However, a critical shift has been made in its development of links with the established health network to broaden its thrust without abandoning its mission. During its existence, the center's definition of its goals and philosophy has changed little. The mechanisms devised to achieve the goals basically are intact. However, over the years, modifications have been made to accommodate growth and change. Some of these can be pinpointed as to time and place, but most have been slow and evolutionary. The board, the leadership, and the staff have responded to the need for changes with creativity and continued commitment to the mission of the organization.

The mechanisms developed and the decisions made by this agency are worthy of attention from other nonprofit service organizations and may be useful in addressing issues related to participatory management, empowerment, effectiveness, and commitment to purpose—all issues addressed directly or indirectly by such organizations.

References

Cates, W., & Rochat, R. W. (1976). Illegal abortions in the United States: 1972–1974. *Family Planning Perspectives, 8,* 86.

Clark, B. R. (1956). Organizational adaptation and precarious values. *American Sociological Review, 21,* 327–336.

Elizabeth Blackwell Health Center for Women. (1975). *Statement of principles.* Philadelphia: Author.

Elizabeth Blackwell Health Center for Women. (1976). *By-laws.* Philadelphia: Author.

Elizabeth Blackwell Health Center for Women. (1993). *Mission statement.* Philadelphia: Author.

Ferguson, K. E. (1984). *The feminist case against bureaucracy.* Philadelphia: Temple University Press.

Gold, R. B. (1990). *Abortion and women's health: A turning point for America?* New York: Alan Guttmacher Institute.

Henshaw, S. K., & Tietze, C. (1986). *Induced abortion: A world review, 1986.* New York: Alan Guttmacher Institute.

Metzendorf, D. D. (1990). *The evolution of feminist organizations: An organizational study.* Unpublished doctoral dissertation, University of Pennsylvania, Philadelphia.

Perlmutter, F. D. (1969). A theoretical model of social agency development. *Social Casework, 50,* 467–473.

Perlmutter, F. D. (1971). Public funds and private agencies. *Child Welfare, 50,* 264–270.

Roe v. Wade, 410 U.S. 113 (1973).

Ruzek, S. B. (1978). *The women's health movement.* New York: Praeger.

Selznick, P. (1957). *Leadership in administration.* New York: Harper & Row.

Stern, P. N. (1986). *Women, health and culture.* Washington, DC: Hemisphere.

Thomas, J. E. (1993, March). *Feminist women's health centers: Internal structures and dynamics.* Paper presented at the Southwestern Social Science Association, New Orleans.

Webster v. Reproductive Health Services, 57 U.S.L.W. 88–605 (1989).

Special appreciation is expressed to Miriam Diamond, Jean Hunt, and Barbara K. Webber for their unstinting cooperation.

INDEX

Health care
 social–political context for, 158–
  160
 women's movement in, 160–161
HMO coverage, 169
Human resources management in
  nonprofit sector, 14
Human Rights Commission (New
  Zealand), 127

I

Iceland, public sector in, 63
Incest. *See* Sexual assault victims
Independent sector, 9
International Organization of
  Jewish Zionist Women
  (WIZO), 97, 105
Israel, 5
 Alcoholic Anonymous, 96
 commercial-private sector, 96
 Counseling Center for Women,
  98–109
 divorce in, 97
 Federation of Israeli Trade
  Unions, 97
 formation of alternative
  organizations, 92–93, 95
 influence of religion, 93
 informal sector, 96
 International Organization of
  Jewish Zionist Women
  (WIZO), 97, 105
 Jewish Agency Foundation, 105–
  106
 marriage and divorce, 97
 Naamat, 97
 Narcotics Anonymous, 96
 New Israel Fund, 105
 private sector, 96
 public sector, 94–95
 self-help organizations, 96
 social-political context, 92–94
 status, problems, and needs of
  women, 97–98

voluntary sector, 94, 96
welfare system, 94–96
Women's forum, 105
women's labor, 97
Women to Women, 105

J

Jewish Agency Foundation (Israel),
  105–106
Joint Committee on Women and
  Employment (New Zealand),
  113

K

King Frederik VII Foundation
  (Denmark), 71
Koop, C. Everett, 160

M

Management roles of nonprofit
  executives
 boards of directors, 13–14
 executive leadership, 11–12
 financial management, 15
 human resources, 14
 policy and planning, 12–13
Marriage
 in Denmark, 69
 in Israel, 97
Medicaid
 funds for abortion, 160
 gynecological services, 173
Men, admittance of, to women's
  centers in Denmark, 70
Ministry of Women's Affairs (New
  Zealand), 127

N

Naamat (Israel), 9
Narcotics Anonymous (Israel), 96

O

Organizational culture, ideal types of, 83
Organizational structure, flat structure as ideal, 140
Otto-Peters, Luisa, 46

P

Patient care, 160–161
Pejnovic, Kata, 47
Policy, definition of, 12
Policy formulation in nonprofit sector, 12–13
Politics, definition of, 12
Private sector in Israel, 96
Public sector
  in Israel, 94–95
  in Scandinavian countries, 63–64
Public Services Association, 113
Puljanke, 57

R

Reintoft, Hanne, 72, 74, 75, 83
Religion
  influence of, in Israel, 93
  social services under auspices of, 9
  and wife battering, 136
Research Fund Administration Committee (RFAC) (New Zealand), 125–126, 127
Residual welfare model, 86
Roe v. Wade, 159, 160

S

Salvation Army (Denmark), 65, 70
SAVENA (New Zealand), 57, 58
Scandinavian welfare states, 62–63
Sexual Assault Task Force, 36–37

Sexual assault victims
  exhibition of paintings and photos by, 105
  services for, in Australia, 24, 28, 36–37
Slobodna rijec, 46
Social services
  characteristics of, 8
  under religious auspices, 9
  responsibility for provision of, 15–16
Socialist Conference of Women of Yugoslavia, 51
Socialist Conference of Yugoslav Women (SCOW), 48
Society for Research on Women in New Zealand (SROW), 110–130
  and advocacy, 123–125
  beginnings and mission, 113, 116–118
  disbanding of national organization, 122
  future, 129–130
  government's effect on, 122
  historical context, 110–116
  interorganizational relationships, 125–127
  leadership, 120
  membership, 120–122
  research studies and advocacy in, 122–125
  structure and governance, 118–120
  threats to, 127–129
Splicanke, 57
State-friendly society, alternative movement in, 153–155
Strategic planning in nonprofit sector, 12
Status of women
  in Denmark, 68–69
  in Israel, 97–98
Supported Accommodation Assistance Programme (SAAP) (Australia), 29

About the Editor

Felice Davidson Perlmutter, PhD, professor of social administration at Temple University, is active in teaching and lecturing on administration of the social services. She is the author of seven books and 70 articles on social administration, social policy, and nonprofit organizations. She is a Fulbright scholar who has extensive international experience as a teacher and researcher.

About the Contributors

Arpad Barath, PhD, is associate professor of health psychology at the Medical School, University of Zagreb. His research interests are in career development, self-help and mutual aid groups, and survey research. He has been a senior fellow at The Johns Hopkins University Institute for Policy Studies and is codirector of a UNICEF-sponsored project on psychosocial help to war-traumatized children.

Ljiljana Bastaic-Barath, MD, is an active teacher and practitioner of Gestalt and family therapy. She is involved in the promotion of women's health programs and services.

Joseph Katan, PhD, is associate professor in the Bob Shapell School of Social Work at Tel Aviv University, Israel. He has published extensively in the fields of social services and social policy.

Kurt Klaudi Klausen, PhD, is associate professor and head of the Department of Commercial Law and Political Science at Odense University, Denmark. He has published books and articles on the internationalization of local government and on the relationship among the public, private, and nonprofit sectors.

Mark Lyons, PhD, is associate professor in the School of Management, University of Technology, Sydney, Australia, and director of the university's Centre for Australian Community Organizations and Management. Dr. Lyons has published in the fields of Australian history, social policy, and nonprofit organizations.

Simi Mizrahi, MSW, is a teacher in the Bob Shapell School of Social Work at Tel Aviv University and a member of The Counseling Center for Women in Tel Aviv.

Kristin Morken is a research assistant at the Department of Comparative Politics, University of Bergen, Norway. Her doctoral research is on the women's shelter movement in Norway.

Julie Nyland is a lecturer in the School of Management, University of Technology, Sydney, Australia. She is an associate of the university's Centre for Australian Community Organizations and Management. She has worked in a variety of nonprofit organizations and as a consultant to government bodies.

Sallie Saunders is a lecturer in the School of Management, University of Technology, Sydney, Australia. She specializes in the management of nonprofit organizations. She has worked in a number of women's community organizations and serves on two ministerial advisory committees on women's homelessness and domestic violence.

Per Selle, PhD, professor of comparative politics at the University of Bergen, Norway, and senior researcher at the Norwegian Center of Organization and Management, is working on a study of the relationship between government and voluntary organizations. He is the author of several books and articles on communism, party organizations, and voluntary organizations.

Miriam Vosburgh, PhD, a New Zealander, has been professor and chair of the Sociology Department at Villanova University. Her research interests are in the field of demography, gender, and the theory and structure of organizations. She was an early member of the Society for Research on Women in New Zealand.

William W. Vosburgh, PhD, is emeritus professor in the Graduate School of Social Work and Social Research of Bryn Mawr College. He has served as director of Research in Public Welfare for the Commonwealth of Pennsylvania. His fields of interest are social welfare policy and formal organizations.

Women & Social Change

Designed by Anne Masters Design

Composed by Wolf Publications, Inc., in Bodoni Book, Eraser Dust, Futura Light, and Futura Condensed

Printed by Gilliland Printing, Inc., on 60# Spectrum